BEYOND——
—HAPPINESS

How You Can Fulfill Your Deepest Desire

FRANK J. KINSLOW

This book is not intended to diagnose, prescribe or treat. The information contained herein is in no way to be considered as a substitute for care from a duly licensed healthcare professional.

BEYOND HAPPINESS

ISBN: 13: 978-0-61522667-9-8
ISBN: 10: 0-6152267-9-5

Cover and interior design by Edge Literary & Marketing Services

Printed in the U.S.A.
Printed October 2008

Dedication

For
Martina

The essence of innocence,
compassion and love.

Contents

Introduction 1

Chapter 1   Who Am I? 7
  I've retired from the game
  Awakening
  Momentum
  What do you want?
  How is "I" different from "me"?
  Now for the good stuff
  ■ *Experience One—How to stop thinking*
  "I am"—The universal healer
  Main Points for Chapter One

Chapter 2   How To See With New Eyes 24
  The ghost of Newton
  When a tree falls in the woods...
  Just a little bit of science
  Two simple rules
  What you expect is what you get
  Extraordinary people
  Mirror vision
  Observation—A full-time job
  Death is life
  Main Points for Chapter Two

Chapter 3   How The Mind Works 34
  Thinking
  Feeling
  Security
  Main Points for Chapter Three

Chapter 4   How Time Works 38
Time is not on my side
Popcorn, pop and pure consciousness
What time is it?—NOW!
What a wonderful discovery you are
Main Points for Chapter Four

Chapter 5   Innerthink.....................................43
Five levels of consciousness
What innerthink is and how it works
Don't mind the mind
Space—The final frontier
■ *Experience Two—Finding unbounded space*
Make time for space
The first crack in the wall of suffering
Spaced out—In a good way
Innerthinking
Pennies from heaven
Main Points for Chapter Five

Chapter 6   How To Fix The Future...........................54
How to overcome anxiety
■ *Experience Three—How to overcome anxiety*
Boredom becomes impossible
The future will take care of itself
Main Points for Chapter Six

Chapter 7   Your Problems Are Not The Problem 59
The homeless mind
Problems do not exist in nature
Appreciating nothing
A watched pot never boils
Main Points for Chapter Seven

Chapter 8   How To Overcome Happiness 66
Ego and the end of fear
Even when ego is happy it is worried
Time plus thought equals fear
Driving Miss Crazy
Fear is a dark, multi-faceted jewel
Feelings and eu-feelings
Fear—The wolf
Happiness—The wolf in sheep's clothing
You cannot control happiness
Great! You've lost all hope
Arjuna and the Song of Life
A side trip to visit God
Back to being hopeless
Main Points for Chapter Eight

Chapter 9   Memory Is Not Intelligent 80
When you think a thought where does it go?
Memory is me
Memory is not intelligent
Memory is always outdated
The three profound advantages of innerthink
Colombia on my mind
Main Points for Chapter Nine

Chapter 10 Fixing A Broken Mind 90
Insanity runs in my family
The cycle of desire
How to create: a silent word from our sponsor
Breaking the addiction of desire
Fixing a broken mind
The menu is not the meal
Anger as a thing
Main Points for Chapter Ten

Chapter 11 Overcoming Psychological Pain 101
The Gate Technique
  ■ *Experience Four—The Gate Technique*
Melting moods
How to mood melt
  ■ *Experience Five—How to overcome negative emotions*
Give me my suffering
Life is like a long car ride
Fear is afraid of dying
Problems are the games we play
Why is a joke funny?
A line drawn in air
Main Points for Chapter Eleven

Chapter 12 Overcoming Physical Pain 118
Fantastic voyage
Mind and body—Hand in glove
The subtle body
Finding your subtle body
  ■ *Experience Six—Finding your subtle body*
Good deeds can make bad things happen
Kiss it and make it better
  ■ *Experience Seven—How to overcome physical pain*
The spiritual scientist
Main Points for Chapter Twelve

Chapter 13 The Perfect Relationship 131
One man's perfect is another man's pain
Perfection is the product of perception
It is impossible to stay in love
What is the purpose of relationships?
The sword and the leaf
But the tigers come at night
Freezing God into form
The ultimate relationship
Main Points for Chapter Thirteen

Chapter 14 How To Not-Know **145**
We know we can but believe we can't
Life as a line in the dirt
The DVD model
The holographic DVD model
One fish, two fish, red fish, blue fish
The dark room
Nothing is not empty
Creation did not happen
Knowledge, knowing and not-knowing
The self cannot exist without the fish
The knower comes and goes with the known
Hold onto your hats—A quick recap (Pun intended.)
■ *Experience Eight—How to not-know*
Main Points for Chapter Fourteen

Chapter 15 When You Become Enlightened **164**
I yam what I yam
Free will and determinism
The problem of free will
Who thought the thought?
It is what it is
Give it a rest
Do we do or do we don't?
When you become self-aware
I am diagonally parked in a parallel universe
You will be astonished
Thanks
Main Points for Chapter Fifteen

Glossary **183**

Bibliography **189**

Introduction

Problems are not the problem

There is a problem that is destroying this world and it has been kept secret from you. Our parents and teachers have unwittingly protected and propagated this secret out of ignorance, not malice. It has survived the generations by a kind of magic and misdirection. If this problem is allowed to continue unchallenged it is quite possible that humankind will disappear from earth in a few generations.

Even the most self-absorbed among us can sense a subtle pulse of insanity threading its way through our everyday existence. We don't have to look as far as the rainforests or the oceans. Damaging environmental forces are at work no farther away than our kitchens and bathrooms. The environment is a grave concern but it is not the problem. Around the globe nations are mistrustful, many openly hostile toward each other. Within the borders of these countries the citizens are restless and discontent. But national and domestic unrest is not the problem. Social structures have become stilted and impersonal. Despite our desperate efforts to deepen family bonds, the family unit continues to disintegrate. As individuals, the weight of this troubled world pressing down on us has yielded an ever-increasing number and variety of physical and psychological illnesses. And still, as a species, we have not exposed the primal problem, the cause of our discontent.

That is the bad news. The good news is that a small number of people, from no specific cultural, educational and economic background or exceptional philosophical and religious influence, have uncovered the culprit. The one element that unifies these people is that they have learned how to neutralize problems by eliminating the "cause" of all our problems. Now, here is the very good news. Their lives have become natural and vibrant expressions of what it means to be human. They are energetic, productive and loving. They are at peace even in the most trying of circumstances. In fact, calm, peace and joy are the necessary expressions of one who is living beyond problems.

It is as if we have been asleep. Our sleep is deep and our dreams delicious. But, dreams are illusions. A wonder-filled life of unimaginable richness awaits us when we awaken. But still we sleep. Life cannot be lived from slumber. The chance to

1

claim our true human heritage is slipping quickly away. A few have already awakened and are trying to rouse the rest of us. If you are asleep, if you have problems, I invite you to awaken to your full stature. Can you find a more immediate or fulfilling labor?

There is a popular definition of insanity that seems to apply particularly well here. It goes something like this, "You are insane when you keep doing things the same way and expect the results to turn out differently." So why is it when we try to do things differently we still end up with the same result, more problems? As we learn to overcome our troubles bigger ones take their place. Not only are our problems multiplying, they are becoming more serious. World war, global warming and "super bugs" caused by overuse of antibiotics threaten our very existence. Our brand of insanity increases with every problem we solve.

Why is that? Why does increased knowledge bring the need for even more knowledge? And why do we feel less in control? More knowledge about our minds, our bodies and our relationships hasn't worked so far. There is an information explosion. Data are streaming in from every corner of the earth, and beyond, at the speed of light. It is increasing exponentially and so are the variety and seriousness of our problems.

Like most people, I have spent most of my life putting out fires, attacking problems by manipulating my environment. I learned many resourceful systems and philosophies to overcome daily dilemma. Learning, of course, is assimilation by the mind. All ideas were welcomed by my mind. Like a fly caught in the web of my mental matrix, each idea was injected with the venom of my ego, the weaver of the web. It was a subtle poison that debilitated but did not kill. Once infected, my ideas seemed sane enough. They should have eliminated problems. But they only created more problems. So I learned more problem-solving techniques. I made more money, I developed new relationships, I became "spiritual." And still my life was overwhelmed with all manner of emergencies, setbacks, difficulties and disasters. Like waves breaking on the beach, problems rolled in one after the other.

Then I realized that information gathering had not and could not abolish my problems. It was here that a very peculiar calm descended on me. I realized that hard work, meticulous planning and good intentions are not the keys to quiescence. In fact, this very realization had brought me more peace than a lifetime of working and planning.

All along I felt that I was not insane because I was always "doing things differently." But when I stepped back and looked at my life the only word I could honestly find to describe it was "insane." My life consisted of long periods of a kind of subliminal "quiet desperation." Then, when the desperation bubbled up to the conscious level, my behavior became frantic and chaotic. I felt as though there wasn't enough time to reach my goals so I could finally be happy. Every now and again happiness would pay me a visit. Times of happiness revolved around an event like buying a new car or coming into a little extra money. When happiness did drop in, however, it was never for long. I would be happy for a few hours or a few days and then it would be weeks or months before it showed up again. It got so I couldn't even enjoy happiness when I had it because I was always worried about loosing it. My life was a simple reflection of the fractured madness we have come to accept as normal living.

The foregoing definition of insanity warns us not to do the same thing and expect different results. When we gather more information and apply it to solve new problems we appear to be doing something different. So that must not be the ultimate source of our problems. What is the ultimate problem? To find the answer we must ask ourselves, "What part of the problem-solving process has always remained the same?"

There is only one aspect of this process that has always been the same: the mind. Every problem must first filter through the mind. The primary problem responsible for all other problems is the mind. Or, more accurately, how the mind works when left unattended. It is a tool. It needs to be guided. It cannot be trusted to run its own affairs. You are not your mind. You are in control of your mind. Or at least you should be. Like Hal, the runaway computer in *2001: A Space Odyssey*, our minds have taken over while we were asleep.

During this "waking-sleep" your mind goes on autopilot. It becomes reflexive and reactive. It does pretty much what it did in the past because you are not consciously there to guide it. Do you see the dilemma? If the mind is running by reflex and memory, how can it fix the problem that presents itself now? If you are asked to do a math problem and you are told that it is addition when it is really a subtraction problem you will get the wrong answer. Your mathematical technique will be perfect but your answer will be wrong. We appear to be working our life's problems just fine but the results just don't add up, at least with any permanency. And when we wonder why things are not working we check our work. As long as we believe it is an addition problem we have no hope of solving it. We do everything right and the answer still comes out wrong.

In life, we are using addition in a subtraction world. No matter how we try to resolve the problems in our lives we can only create more: more suffering, more pain and more destruction. We look around and see that everyone else is doing what we are doing so we must be right. All we can do is rationalize that humans were meant to suffer. "Humans always have and always will," we tell ourselves in an effort to soothe our deeply troubled souls. But this does not explain those aberrations of humanity who rise above suffering to tell us that we can, and must, do the same. Yes, we were taught a lie by our parents, our teachers and our leaders as they were taught by theirs. But that lie can be healed in the heartbeat of a generation.

A single fundamental truth has been missed. It is a simple truth that is easily overlooked by our minds. I found it only after more than 40 years of searching and then only by negation, by subtraction if you will. It is a simple truth that I will share with you in this book. I do not consider myself an authority or particularly learned on this subject. Nor do I have any special talents or gifts that have enabled me to be any more successful than you will be. Inner peace, the freedom from problems, is the birthright of all of us. I am simply sharing what I have learned. I do not feel that I am finished unfolding the wonder that is my life. In fact, the writing of this book has opened me to deeper and fuller expressions of the bliss and love that is my Self. In writing, the hours and weeks washed over me like an ocean deep and silent. I wrote this book first of all for me. But I had you in mind all the time.

The focus of this book

Beyond Happiness is a poignant and practical guide to personal inner peace. It clearly identifies what peace is, why it is so rarely experienced, why it is vital to our continued existence and how it can be realized without a change in lifestyle. Because it is unique amongst the myriad self-help and spiritually oriented books, it combines the three major methods of teaching in a single, simple presentation broadening its appeal and increasing its effectiveness. The single parent, a CEO, saint or sinner could pick up a copy of *Beyond Happiness* and within minutes experience inner peace.

We are frequently reminded that money can't buy happiness. But it is my experience that money does buy happiness. So does sex, religion and position. Happiness however, is conditional. The conditions are determined by the individual. Earning a hundred dollars a day would make a poor man happy and a rich man cry. What makes us happy today may cause sorrow tomorrow. Receiving a promotion can bring with it stressors that far outweigh the raise in salary and status. Once achieved, happiness all too quickly evaporates into the mist of memory, forcing us to live in the past.

Peace is unconditional. It is everywhere, all the time. Money can't buy peace. Neither can peace be realized by hard work, strong will nor long hours of spiritual austerities. We are living under a perfidious misunderstanding. It is peace, not happiness, that quells the fires of desire and leaves the heart truly content. Peace is the very essence of emotion and thought and yet beyond the touch of both.

Sustained inner peace is rare. Even the most fleeting glimpse is unknown to many. There is almost universal confusion about what it is or if it has any practical value. Few realize that inner peace is a symptom of how we perceive our Self. The Self is the foundation upon which all thoughts, feelings and actions originate. The unbounded unchanging Self is the progenitor of peace. This is the secret, the final mystery.

How does this book work?

Beyond Happiness exposes this secret in a unique way. It approaches the singularity of Self from many different perspectives, drawing on your experience and thus stimulating your interest. The paradox of teaching inner peace is that it can not be taught. However, there is a way around this apparent incongruity. Each principle for finding peace is introduced to you by stimulating both intellect and heart. This method embraces both the right and left-brain reader. Traditionally obtuse spiritual teachings are demystified and broken into simple logical language. Anecdotes, analogies, humor and heart-warming stories are designed to draw you deeper into the material while creating a more animated bond with the book. The third prong of the trident is the actual experience of peace provided by interactive exercises. Self-awareness cannot be taught, but by using the unique method of Not-Knowing, supported by eight inner exploration "experiences" your awareness is gently and continually brought back to Self. This threefold process of unfolding the heart, mind and experience runs quietly in the background. Up front, it generates a sense of fun, lighthearted exploration and the quiet excitement of uncovering deeper expressions of your Self.

But how do we resolve the paradox that peace cannot be taught? Technique is a bridge to be left behind once the obstacle is crossed. Belief in technique keeps us dependent on technique, and inner peace must blossom free of dependency. Holding to technique would be like walking back and forth over the bridge whenever inner peace is desired. Permanent peace becomes impossible. As you progress through the pages of *Beyond Happiness* you are invited to give up your reliance on technique. It is built into both text and exercise. When you finish this book you will experience inner peace without reliance on teacher or technique.

Finally, breaking free of technique quickly leads to what I call "momentum." Momentum is characterized by an intuitive regeneration of peace when it is lost. It is the experience of those who strive after inner peace that the very effort pushes it even further from their grasp. In times of trauma peace is lost completely, obscured by a vortex of abhorrent emotions and unyielding thoughts. After momentum dawns, when inner peace is lost it is automatically reestablished without effort or forethought. At this point life's thorny problems can not stick and living becomes more free and frictionless.

Beyond Happiness is written in common simple language. It is a workbook without the work. This matter-of-fact approach to traditionally profound or obtuse principles keeps your mind fertile while the exercises remove clutter and increase mental clarity. I make a concentrated effort to define pivotal words that may cause confusion. Make sure you frequently refer to the glossary. You will find it of great assistance in easing your transition to momentum.

I will never ask you to take my word on faith. I encourage you to draw from your own experience and empirically test the concepts in question by performing the related exercises in the book. Only then will you be able to break down the mystery of the Self into bite-size pieces easily digested. This one-two punch of providing a clear understanding and supporting it with a relevant and significant experience affords you an animated and direct experience of your Self.

Please accept my invitation to read this book and share its message with others. It is an innocent invitation to join in the celebration of life. It is an offering from one heart to another, from Self to Self.

Frank Kinslow   **Sarasota, Florida**   **New Year's Day, 2005**

CHAPTER 1
Who Am I?

"I yam what I yam."
Popeye the Sailorman

I've retired from the game

I've never completely sold out to adulthood. I remember the bliss of drawing with a stick in the dirt or watching clean white clouds slide slowly across a deep cerulean sky. Or watching in wonder as a dewdrop struggled with each sympathetic breeze to break free from a spider's web. The child's eye is the saint's eye.

I have always felt that childhood and adulthood should not be at war with each other. I felt this as a child, in training for adulthood. Most of us give in, you know? Then we forget. We are seduced by the sheer power of becoming an adult. I was a child in post-WWII Japan. I was 10 years old when I first became aware of the battle between the innocence of being and the accountability of control. It happened like this:

I had taken up the sport of Judo. Early every evening after dinner with my family, I left for the do-jo with my rolled judo-gi uniform hanging over my shoulder by its brown belt. I walked past small dimly lit houses that crowded over the narrow twisted streets of Yokohama like neighbors over the backyard fence collecting the last crumbs of gossip before darkness demanded silence. Thin gray smoke from the wood-burning hibachi stoves stretched out in the still air like spirit snakes. Hanging motionless, they would breathe in the darkness then rise, stealing slowly across the wooden shingled roofs. Soon the Soba-man would come. And like a fisherman's net thrown on still waters, the soulful sound of the noodle vender's "Soooo-baaaa" settled into the houses, gathering the thoughts of the dwellers within like so many silver fishes. I would turn from the street onto one of the scores of tangled footpaths that separated the houses. In a few steps I would find a courtyard with a small garden and the house where I learned Judo from my master.

Sensei was one of four 10th-degree black belts in the world at the time, the highest recognition in the sport. Although I felt it, I did not know until sometime later that he was a man inspired by peace. He did not speak much but when he did, his peace penetrated more deeply than his thoughts.

My peace, on the other hand, was waning. I was in training for adulthood. As an American, I was bigger than my Japanese counterparts. Instead of technique, I preferred to use force to subdue my opponents. One evening sensei built me up as the strongest in the class. That night I was to randori (competitive practice) with a boy who came up to just above my navel. Full of recent accolades, I felt confident of the outcome. I remember to this day the vision I had of how I would win the match. I planned to make an intricate and rather exotic move, catapulting this half-pint through the paper window and out into the courtyard. But fortunately for me, it did not happen at all as I had planned. It is a painful story, so I'll keep it short. My slippery little opponent repeatedly refused my offer to leave class early via the side window—in fact he made a counter offer I couldn't refuse. I remember looking at the ceiling quite a few times that evening. Though not at all a part of my original thinking, I was somehow getting used to the idea. I think the behavioral modification people would call it "reconditioning." My back and the mat, heretofore veritable strangers, were becoming old friends. Although the match probably only lasted 10 minutes, it seemed to take 10 hours. All those present in the dojo were politely hiding their smiles while Tsunami Devil, as I had come to call him, and I bowed to end the match. To rub salt in fresh wounds, one of the other students told me that the boy was only six years old. I hadn't seen him in the dojo before, nor would I again. I think he was a ringer. I am certain his sole purpose was to make the rounds to the different dojos and humble overinflated egos dressed in judo attire.

The very next night, which I had contemplated missing all together, sensei taught us the Belly Water System. It was a mind-over-matter technique that increased the strength of the body by quieting the mind. As I practiced the technique, the anger and humiliation I had been carrying inside since the night before drained like water from a broken vessel. I was empty. What took its place was a calm presence that just seemed to observe what I was doing. I had been reunited with my Self. In that presence I was safe, complete. I felt the kind of unshakable peace that comes from no other source. I remember it so clearly because of the contrast. I went from feeling anger and frustration to being surrounded by a quiet inner strength. It took only seconds. Looking back I am sure this was all by sensei's design.

This peace stood out clearly in my mind for another reason. I hadn't been having much of it by that age. The wonder of life was fading. I was already succumbing to the promise of power through force. My parents, teachers and even my peers were showing me that if I wanted to get what I desired, or what they desired for me, I would have to practice self-discipline, exercise great presence of will and work very hard. The fly in the ointment was that I had just rediscovered the peaceful power of childhood and I liked it. On one side I had playful presence nipping at my heels. On the other, I had the assurance that I would be successful beyond my wildest dreams if I could only learn to control myself and my environment.

A half century has passed since I rediscovered peace in that Yokohama dojo. And I have learned to control my environment, but not as I was encouraged to do by my teachers. I let my Self do that for me now. I've retired from the game.

Awakening

Peace, I have discovered, is a symptom. It is the result of neither understanding nor effort. For most, it comes altogether too infrequently and always when unlooked for—that is—if you do not know how to look for it.

We will uncover the secret of finding inner peace as we pass through the pages of this book. I have devoted my adult life to the pursuit of peace. I spent years in silent meditation, literally sequestered on mountaintops in exotic and faraway lands. I dedicated several hours of each typical day to meditation, to finding and holding on to peace. After 35 years of devoted "spiritual" work I was no closer to enjoying sustained inner peace than when I had started my journey. Despondent and frustrated I finally gave up the cause. I gave up everything that defined my life and found only a desert in its place. There was no peace there either. I had just the faintest spark of hope left.

One day while sitting in the Borders bookstore café in Flint, Michigan, and staring into a Styrofoam cup of tasteless green tea, the last ember of hope winked out. When it died, nothing moved. The universe had stopped breathing. Barely perceptible within that stillness was a pinpoint of peace. As my awareness was drawn to it, I felt like Alice falling down the rabbit hole. As I fell I become smaller like a pebble thrown off a high bridge. Just before I winked out, there was an explosion. It felt like the Big Bang except instead of fire and stone, there was peace. The force of the explosion filled my universe with stone solid peace.

Sitting there at the table, the sun broke through the clouds warming my back and the cafe filled with chattering while a jazz CD played overhead. I sat still, cradling in my hands the cup of lukewarm tea. Everything was exactly as before except the room was now filled with a clear and vibrant light, the face of peace. How the entire universe had poured into that little café already overflowing with bodies and books, I cannot say. But it was there, and nobody noticed. Galaxies and the stuff of creation passed effortlessly through our bodies, and still nobody noticed. My breath was not moving, but tears streamed down my face, falling on the table on either side of the cup. A young student studying with her friends at the next table met my gaze, then quickly turned away.

As if by some unseen cue, my consciousness shrank to an infinitesimal wrinkle in a shimmering burst of energy, smaller than the smallest sub-atomic particle. I watched as clouds of raw energy congealed and converged with other clouds. From these amorphous vapors sprang the animate souls of trees and seas and the fertile earth, only to dissolve back into energy without form. I was everywhere, greater than the greatest and smaller than the smallest.

As those swirling energies of creation faded, I again found myself back in the mundane present we confidently call the "real world." Immediately the people and music, the smells of coffee and toasted bagel swam back into my awareness. They were anything but mundane. My tears were drying, I saw more clearly. Everything appeared crisp and clean and lighted from within. All form was energy here, too. But there was something hidden deep within the finest form of energy. It was unknowable but I was aware of It. It was intelligent and aware. Most of all it was compassionate—no, It was Compassion. And, somehow, I was It.

Momentum

The intensified state of inner peace and bliss lasted for 5 weeks or so. As I went about my daily chores I found a kind of effortlessness had crept into my routine. I sometimes felt separate from things, as if peace had lifted me above the din, and yet I was so fully a part of all that has been created as to be one with it. I don't believe this transformation was observable by family or friends. It was every bit as subtle as it was profound. I don't think the intensity diminished so much as it was assimilated. I got used to it, and everything seemed normal, as before—except for one thing: something so wonderfully delicious and completely normal that I wrote this book to tell you about it.

Since that day, I no longer have to search for peace. Yes, I lose it, sometimes for the greater part of a day, sometimes longer. But it always comes back. And it does so without any effort on my part. Inner peace returns to me like a child returns to his mother when he has been too long away. We embrace as parent and child and continue on together, not minding so much the rigors of the routine world.

I call this spontaneous return of peace "momentum." It means that struggle and frustration, anxiety and discontent are winding down, losing their hold on you. Negative forces, starved of the tumultuous emotions that sustain them, become harmless specters. Normally when we are upset we can stay that way for days or months, or even years. Your mind becomes preoccupied with the problem, rehashing the offending event and rehearsing scenarios in your mental court of law. Your mind is overtaken by thought, missing the tenderness each moment presents. Actually, runaway thinking does not need a precipitous event to draw the mind away from this moment. Have you ever driven to work and remembered almost nothing about the drive itself? While it was otherwise occupied, your body and your car drove your mind to work. You might say that there is nothing worth noting on the way to work anyway, but that is not the point. And, you would be wrong. This autothinking is a problem. More accurately, it is a symptom of something that is deeply wrong.

That is why I have written this book. First, I would like to interest you in discovering your own inner peace. You have a simple choice, peace or problems. Ultimately that is your only choice. Second, I would like you to know how simple it is to be at peace. You do not need to devote your life to finding it as I did. That is actually the perfect way to insure that you don't find peace. I would like you to experience first hand how peace eliminates problems, allowing you to enjoy the richness and the beauty that is your life. Finally, I want you to reach momentum. When peace effortlessly perpetuates itself in your life my work is done. So, before we go to the actual experience of peace, let's take a look at two questions that must be answered.

What do you want?

At first glance the question, "What do you want?" seems innocent enough. Wanting is automatic. It appears pretty simple really. A desire comes and you want the object of that desire. If you're hungry you want food. If you are lonely you want companionship. But where do these desires come from? Some we know come from physical or psychological needs like thirst and love. Others don't seem to have a particular need attached to them. You might, for instance, want the red convertible sports car instead of the more practical family sedan. Or, how about the desire for buns of steel when the ones you presently possess are fully functional? What causes this "wanting without needing" desire that can be so unsettling, and ultimately so destructive?

If you take the time to explore this simple question with me, I promise you that your life will change not a little, but profoundly and in the most genuinely sincere ways. You will discover a hidden world just beyond your thoughts. This is no shadow world or reflection of other realms you already know. The world beneath the question is deep and wide and pure. It is the world from which your present life draws its breath. It is the final answer to the question "What do you want?"

This book can open many exciting doors for you, but in the end there is only a single door you need walk through. It is not necessary to look beyond this single insight. You may need some preparation before you can walk through that door but that is easily remedied. There's lots of work to be done and even more fun to be had. You are about to embark on a voyage, not from here to there, but rather from here to hear. You will come to realize that to be complete, you do not need to go anywhere. Nor need you do anything! This voyage might better be thought of as an expansion, a kind of perceptual opening that ends with the realization that life is already perfect.

If this statement seems fantastic or unbelievable then get ready for a wild ride. Come along with me and you will discover for yourself the remarkable life you have been missing. You will uncover the science of seeing and the art of being. There are no problems in nature. Only humans make problems. When a human sees his or her true nature, problems dissolve like the sun melting into a placid sea.

In the beginning you will be invited to learn in the same way you have throughout your life, in a linear, goal-oriented manner. Generally we are in the habit of manipulating things which results in some amount of control over our environment. That is the normal way, but not the natural way. And it has its dangers. There is another broader means of living that includes the goal-oriented behavior but far exceeds it in scope. This is a kind of functioning that comes not from the mind, but beyond it. While it is impossible to explain, it is easily experienced once the proper rules are applied. The art of "being" will blossom automatically as you continue to read this book. You will see it in the ease and joy that begins to seep into your daily life. Time will slide effortlessly by and problems will lose their grip on you. Your appreciation of even the most mundane experiences will at times overwhelm you, filling you with gratitude and joy. Like a child in love with the world you will begin to see through the eyes of innocence.

Your experience will always keep up with your understanding, making your knowledge complete. For instance, when I introduce the concept that peace can be found between your thoughts, it is only fair that I show you how to experience that inner peace for yourself. You will not have to take anything that I say on faith. You will prove me right or wrong by your own experience when you perform the exercises. And while we are on the subject of these designated exercises I call experiences, it might be well to take a look ahead to see what is in store for you as you progress through the book.

In the first experience you will learn how to stop your thinking. It is offered as an illustration to support the point that you are not your thoughts. You still exist even when your mind is silent. While this experience is used to demonstrate a point it is also exceptionally functional. If you do no more than practice this first exercise (and don't worry if you have previously tried to clear you mind of thought but failed. You will have no trouble doing it this time.), you will find yourself enjoying more energy and better health along with enhanced moments of intimacy with family and friends. And that's just the first exercise. There are seven more that will show you how to boost your immune system, reduce stress-related conditions like digestive difficulties and high blood pressure and increase energy and mental clarity. But more importantly you will learn to overcome physical and emotional pain and the fear of death and you will learn to eventually eliminate problems.

If you are getting a little excited about this knowledge then hold onto your hat. Overcoming pain and eliminating problems is just the fluff. Make no mistake these experiences are invaluable for achieving specific results. If it is the mastery of life you are after then you must step away from doing and learn to be. And that is what I am here to tell you. The underlying theme of this book is this: Being is more effective than doing. If you want to have the ultimate joy and peace that life has to offer you cannot *do* anything to get it. The wholeness of life is beyond the pieces. No matter how much money or power or how many friends we have, we can never get enough to be completely happy. For that we must have inner peace. When we learn new skills or develop new relationships we do so with the idea that we will control more of our environment. In our minds, more control means more happiness. Somewhere deep inside is the hope that if we can control enough of our world we will attain permanent happiness. This is a dangerous misconception and much of this book is devoted to dispelling the illusion. Controlling the parts in an effort to control the whole has never worked. Do you know anyone who is always happy? I rest my case.

What is happiness anyway? Is it what we are truly striving for or is that too a delusion? I will deal with this in detail later but for now it is important to know that happiness is not what we ultimately want. It is not our deepest desire. Happiness is part of the problem, not the cure. Happiness, like that red sports car, is what you desire, not what you need. As you will see, no matter how successful you are at finding it, happiness will never bring you what you really need. Happiness depends on conditions. If the conditions line up in accordance with your definition of happiness, then you are happy. If they don't completely fall into place, then you are less happy. And you are unhappy if things don't go your way. Have you ever noticed that the harder you struggle to hold onto happiness the less of it you actually seem to have? Why is that? Why is happiness so fleeting?

We are happy when things go right. But how often do events live up to our expectations? When we look back over a lifetime, it is easy to see that the times we were really happy were but momentary peaks. Those brief peaks of happiness are surrounded by the persistent and repetitive flatlands of the common life. Sure, we nurture a subtle sense of accomplishment when we are able to snare happiness, however briefly. It becomes a kind of assurance that we really are O.K. and that things are going to get even better. But we almost never look beyond this fragile sense of contentment, afraid of the unknown forces that are brewing deeper in the mind, just beyond the light. Doing so would disturb that delicate illusion we work so hard to maintain. Fortunately, we don't have to swim forever in those murky waters.

The impermanent nature of happiness is a great teacher. But I am afraid we have been poor students. We have fallen asleep in class. That single lesson is being repeated over and over and over again. And still we blissfully snore away our lives as just a hint of spittle gathers at the corner of our mouths. When we do awaken, we will realize that the single lesson to be learned is this: Being is freedom. Doing without first being is bondage. Being is the simple act of not-doing. Not-doing means that we first become aware of our Self and then watch as our world is created through the Self. Knowing the Self effortlessly dissolves problems and the sufferings that accompany them. The result is inner peace and prosperity beyond any dream.

Inner peace is a result of being. By being I mean being aware. "Well," you say, "I am already aware." Yes, that is true enough. You are aware of thinking this and doing that. But are you aware of your Self? "Of course," you answer indignantly, "I am aware that I am reading this book. I am also aware of my body and that I have a job and a family." Those things make up what I call "me." They are the particulars of your individual life. Your Self is not at all the same. As you will see, your Self is indescribable and indestructible. Being aware of your Self adds that element of indestructibility to your existence. When you are indestructible you lose all reason for worry and inner peace dawns. It's just that simple. The outcome of becoming aware of your Self has to be inner peace. Inner peace is a symptom of problem-free living. But it is much, much more.

As you continue through this book a remarkable change will begin to take place within you. In the beginning you may want to learn how to specifically quell disturbing emotions or overcome your fear of death. I encourage that, at least initially. Learning in this way is like fighting a battle. The plan of attack is to conquer the problem with knowledge and technique. There is nothing wrong with enlisting a specific approach to remove some form of provocation but you must not think that you can ever know or do enough to be free of problems or free in peace. You may not have a comprehensive understanding of inner peace or may not even care if you do. Either way, it doesn't matter. This is a very intimate journey that only you can take. I have no plans for you. I have discovered a way of living that includes the "normal" life but enriches it beyond belief. It is my intention to meet with you where you are comfortable. While there is only one door, there are many paths leading to that door. I will approach the single lesson from different perspectives, allowing you to choose which ones you feel most comfortable with. I will show you how a slight shift in your perception will release your tendency to struggle, replacing it with a fluid ease that embraces life rather than clashing with it. Nothing is given up except fear and suffering. It is a pure life that all are able to live if they so choose. In fact, your deepest desire, the one from which all other desires spring, is to "Know Thy Self ." That is the starting point and the final destination. As you proceed from chapter to chapter I will never let you forget that. Not only is it the driving theme of this book but it is also the underlying current of life.

So far I have asked a lot of questions and only hinted at some of the answers. They are coming. There are a couple of points we must first consider but in a few more pages you will be offered your first "experience" of Self. Make sure that you are faithful to the exercises so that your experience is fertile. I want these words to come alive for you and the only way that can happen is if you hear the music for which the lyrics were written.

How is "I" different from "me"?

Words have more impact on us than we normally give them credit for. I like to be very clear about what a word means and how it is used. Many people have the unrewarding and ultimately destructive habit of taking a position on an issue without clearly defining the pivotal words they use. For instance, a woman will ask her man,"Do you love me?"He answers, "Yes, very much."And off they skip down the highway of bliss, each believing love is the same for both of them. If ignorance is bliss, they will not remain ignorant for long. Their relationship will force them to examine what it means to love, or it will slowly erode from the inside. Do you doubt that many people take firm stands on wobbly words? Ask a friend to explain in some detail the words "friend" or "terrorist" or even to describe the taste of a banana. It can be a very eye-opening exercise. Her description is guaranteed to be different, possibly significantly different, from your own definitions. We fall into the habit of thinking that other people see things the same way we do when, in fact, that is never the case. The one thing that can be said about people is that everyone is different. Our perspective on the world is completely unique, shared by no other being. We are relative beings. At least that is the way we live our lives. We live as if there is no foundation, no common point of reference that holds true for all humans. We are like specks of dust floating aimlessly in a dimly lit room.

If there were a universal point of reference what do you suspect it might be? Would it be outer space or inner space, within the mind or beyond it? Well, it just so happens that there is a single point of reference shared by all of humanity. It is common not only to humans but to all life, all creation. It is the stuff of the sages.

It is the Self. (Note: The meaning of the words Self, "I" and "I Am" are interchangeable and give us a chance to view this single concept of Self from different, more enlightening perspectives.)

Our basic nature, the Self, is impossible to experience with our senses. We can't see, taste or smell it. The mind can think *about* it, but we are helpless when it comes to *thinking* it. Those are mental processes and Self eludes the probing fingers of the mind. Self has no form, nothing for those mental digits to grab hold of. Every thought and thing comes from Self and yet it has no substance, nothing for the senses to appreciate or for the mind to embrace.

Is this getting a little too abstract for you? Stick with me on this. It will be well worth your time. Your mind is just having trouble trying to examine something that cannot be examined. But it can be experienced. And that is coming up.

Even though your Self has no substance, it is continually sustaining and protecting you. Self is like a warm coat in winter. Even if you are busy with the business of living and have forgotten that you are wearing the coat, it is still keeping you warm. It does not matter if you do not completely grasp the concept of Self. It is far harder to talk about than to experience. In fact, Self can be experienced even if you have never heard of it. The experience of Self is exceedingly subtle and sublime. Chances are you have already been with your Self and not even known it. And that is a problem. If you are unaware of the Self, you cannot know your deepest desire. In the next few pages I will hand over the keys that will open the door to Self. The only prerequisites are that you are a human and you are conscious. That's all it takes. Self-discovery is your birthright.

Why is it important to be aware of your Self? It's more than important, it is vital. To "Know Self" is to become free of hopes and fears. That's what happens. When you "Know Thy Self", as Socrates encouraged us to do so long ago, your security becomes unshakable. Then your feelings become strong and positive and your thinking is clear and decisive. In addition, your senses (hearing, sight, taste, etc.) become sharper and more vibrant. And your body will age more slowly. It becomes relaxed, languid and far more resistant to stress and disease. Not bad dividends for such a simple discovery.

Take a moment and think back to your childhood, and then re-visit some part of your adolescence. Now, remember a time during your twenties, thirties, etc., until you reach your present age. Think about what you are doing right now. Over your lifetime your interests and feelings have changed, your body has grown and aged, family has matured and friends have come and gone. But there was a part of you that was with you as far back as you can remember and is with you still today. It has remained unchanged.

When you said, "I want my mommy," "I hate gym class," "I will love you forever," or "I don't like loud music" you were identifying things, events and feelings that were happening to "me" but not to "I." The things and feelings of your life like wanting mommy, hating gym class, etc., all changed and now reside in that part of our past called the memory. Things changed but "I" did not.

When you say, "I am hungry," you are identifying both sides of your existence, the unchanging "I" and the changeable "me." You are saying that the "I" part of you is observing the "me" part of you being hungry. "I" is like a silent witness just enjoying the scenery of your life. "Me" is the scenery. "I" has always been with you, and has not aged or changed in any other way. Alfred Lord Tennyson spoke to this mystery of enduring changelessness in his poem, *The Brook* when he penned, "Men may come and men may go, but I go on forever." We could just as easily, but far less eloquently say my security, feelings, thoughts, body and environment may come and go but "I" go on forever. It certainly is not as stirring to the soul, but it does get the point across.

The senses and the body are like horses pulling a chariot through life. The mind is that chariot. "I" is the passenger, the witness to all that is happening. It remains unaffected and free from the forces of our world. It is the still center of peace. It is our shelter from the raging storm that is life. "I" is another name for Self.

"Me" is ever changing and "I" never changes. Although the mind seems to know where it is going it really is lost with out "I." "I" is like the Global Positioning Satellite, it doesn't *do* anything but without it the mind has no point of reference. When we do not have awareness of "I" we are swept away by the mind, body and senses, the components of "me." The horses and chariot run away with the passenger. During those rare times when, for a few valued moments, we are able to keep the chaotic world at bay, we may find ourselves asking, "What does it all mean?" or "What is my purpose for being?" And, when no answer comes from "me", we escape through overworking, television, drugs, sex, making money, spending money or anything else that will divert the mind from those uncomfortable quiet moments. The answer is simple. As soon as we become aware of "I", a kind of stillness comes over us. "I", the Self, is first felt as a gentle peace. In time, when peace becomes stronger, joy and a sense of awe enter our awareness. The feeling is like watching a beautiful sunset but no sun is needed. Nothing is needed. Peace and joy begin showing up at the most peculiar times and in the most peculiar places. One day you will be amazed to find inner peace showing up right in the middle of some traumatic event like an argument or an emergency at work. Peace, the result of Self-awareness begins to intermingle with non-peace. It is the blending of "I" and "me" that deepens the life experience and broadens our view of the world.

When we become aware of our Self we become like an ocean. At the bottom it is still and silent. On the surface we find foam and bubbles and waves. The unpredictable, ever-changing surface is like "me." "I" resembles the quiet depths.

However, even the greatest wave is still made of water. The silent water at the depths we call "I" and the tumultuous water on the surface we call "me." In the final analysis, it is all water. "Me" is simply an active expression of "I." Living only on the surface of the ocean means we identify with turbulence and change. We rise and fall with our hopes and fears only to be dashed on the rocky shores of illusion. Simply by becoming aware of the depths of "I" we effortlessly enjoy stability and serenity. The storms of the surface still rage on, but from the vantage point of "I" we remain untouched.

Another way we can refer to "I" is by saying, "I Am." By saying it this way, we are pointing out that "I" doesn't do anything, it just is. "I Am" means that only "I" exists, nothing more. I like using "I Am" because it has a tendency of deepening the sense of "I." Renee Descartes, the celebrated 17th century French philosopher, is best known for saying, "I think, therefore I am." Oddly enough, Renee had it backwards. If you'll pardon the pun, he had "de-cart before de-horse." He should have said, "I Am, therefore I think." If we follow Descartes' reasoning, then when he stopped thinking he would no longer exist. That simply is not so. This reasoning would make sense to someone who is always thinking, surviving only on the surface of the ocean of Self. But what would happen if your thoughts just stopped? Would you really become nonexistent? Would you just turn off as if some fateful finger flipped your light switch? I say no-no. And I will prove it to you in the next section.

When you say, "I am hungry"you are acknowledging both the changing and the unchanging aspects of your being. I Am + hungry = "I" + "me." Normally we devote all our attention to the hungry "me" and ignore the flavor of "I." Satisfying only the carnal hunger, you will still leave the table famished for the fullness of "I." Both sides of the equation must be addressed. Your problems will not disappear, and peace will not flourish until you become aware of your Self.

You are about to discover that when you stop thinking, the mind will cease to exist but "I" goes on forever. So, when the thought of hunger disappears, all that is left is I Am. When anger dies away, there only exists I Am. All worldly turmoil dissolves into the boundless embrace of "I," the wholeness of Self. And when the mind and body resurface as the wave of "me," they draw deeply from the ocean of "I."

Now for the good stuff

An identity founded on change means never being completely at rest. That means you really never know your real nature. Your Self is the part of you that never changes. Let me say that again. Your Self is *unchanging*. Take a moment to think about that. This is not a philosophy nor is it fanciful thinking. It is more concrete than a stone. Your Self does not age, get tired or suffer fear or pain. When you come to know Self completely you will no longer suffer or be hurt by others. How can this happen? All that is needed is just a slight shift in perception. This perceptual shift can be made quickly, easily and with little effort. All the talk in the world will never get us any closer to the experience. The key to opening the adult heart and releasing the innocence of the inner child is learning to pay attention to what you are doing right NOW! You have everything you need, so let's get started.

Experiencing I Am is the essence of simplicity; however, it may take several times for you to get the hang of it. Not because you can't do it, but because you may at first be looking for something different. Not to worry, it is a natural human function and everyone can do it. Just be easy and follow the simple directions and you will soon be shaking hands with your Self.

Several great teachers in the 20th century used this technique to stop thinking. It is a direct approach, not needing thought or meditation. Here's how it goes:

Experience One
How to stop thinking

Sit comfortably and close your eyes. Just follow your thoughts wherever they may lead you. Don't guide them or judge them. Simply watch them come and go. After you have watched your thoughts for 5 or 10 seconds, ask yourself this question, "Where will my next thought come from?" Then be very alert to see what happens. Just wait and watch.

What did happen? Was there a short break in your thinking while you waited for the next thought? Did you notice a space, a kind of gap between the question and the next thought? O.K., reread the instructions and perform the exercise again. I'll wait...

There, did you notice a slight hesitation in your thinking, a pause...between thoughts? If you were alert after you asked "Where will my next thought come from?" you will have noticed that your mind was just waiting for something to happen. The momentary break in your thinking is the mind trying to decide what to think next. Tolle says it is like a cat watching a mouse hole. You were awake, waiting, but there were no thoughts in that gap. Please do this exercise several more times and pay attention to the gap, the space between thoughts. It may be very fleeting but it will be there. Once you become aware of this mental pause, it will get wider, deeper and longer.

You have experienced this gap many times before but I'll bet you haven't paid much attention to it. When your mind is "me" it is not interested in stillness. On one level it considers stillness counter productive. The mind abhors a vacuum. At the very least your mind considers the gap a nuisance, something that must be filled.

Don't most of us get a little embarrassed or rattled when we can't think of what we want to say? It's right on the tip of our tongue, but no matter how hard we try, we can't get the answer out? The harder we try, the deeper that word gets buried. When does the answer come? It comes when we stop whipping our thoughts into a frenzy and allow them to settle down. As soon as we stop trying and become quiet, or begin thinking of something else, the word flies out of our mouth as if it were shot from a cannon. The wayward word did not come from the active mind. It came from the depths of the silent Self.

Here's what I mean. If someone asks you your name, you answer without hesitation. The response is sure and automatic. When you are asked what you had for breakfast there is a short gap in your thinking while your mind looks for an answer. If the question is more difficult, the mind will take longer to produce the answer. What this means is, the mind is waiting for the answer to take form out of that silence. You see, the mind does not create answers. It does not create anything. It only reflects what is created in the Self. This is a very bitter pill for the mind to swallow for it has fallen in love with the illusion that it is the creator.

Our mind, always in a hurry to own the answer, becomes impatient with what appears as wasted time. Constant mental activity is a smoke screen. It tries to cover up the fact that creation comes from stillness and not from activity. It wants to grab on to the answer and start using it to gain more control. The inattentive mind is wasteful and hurtful.

When you ask your mind, "Where will my next thought come from?" it is forced to stop and pay attention. Its natural tendency is to take the first thought that pops up and run with it. But if you resist this tendency to be "productive" and watch to see where your next thought really comes from, you will be rewarded with a glimpse of your Self, the pause that refreshes. You have just found the answer to the question "What do you want?" It is the answer to our original question "What is my deepest desire?" The spawn of all other desires and the torment of the ever-restless mind is that profoundly deep longing to know thy Self.

Now that you know where thoughts come from, I recommend that you do this simple experience for one minute, once every hour. Take a minute at some time during every hour and stop your thinking. (If this is impractical, then do it when you can for longer periods such as 5, 10 or even 20 minutes. Shorter, more frequent visits to Self are more valuable for our purposes.) When other thoughts push their way in, don't fight them. This will always happen because it is the nature of the mind to think. Just keep reintroducing the question with *complete aware-ness*, until your time has passed. Be consistent and you won't be sorry. At first you will probably have to close your eyes, but very quickly you will be able to do it with eyes open. Soon thereafter you will be able to have this experience while driving, conversing with a neighbor or in the middle of an urgent project for work. It won't take long for you to realize how life-changing this innocent experience can be. You won't have to do any more than to observe the gap between your thoughts on a regular basis; the rest will be taken care of for you. You will become more relaxed, creative, energetic and friendly. In a few days you will feel a deeper sense of peace. In a few more days the experience will come without effort. When it does, it is important to keep to your schedule of one minute an hour and look on the spontaneous visits from Self as a blessing. After some time you will reach momentum, the point at which peace automatically renews itself when lost. Now all you need do is sit back and enjoy the ride.

Here is a quick review. When we forget the Self, we forget that thoughts are created out of "I Am." When this happens we identify with our thoughts and feelings. When we say, "I am angry," we align ourselves with the anger. Then we are attached to whatever the anger brings—hurt, frustration, revenge, etc. It is just a short step from there that we enter into a heavyweight wrestling match with our thoughts and feelings. It is a match we cannot win. The problem is that we think we are our minds, and that gets us into big trouble.

The mind is a product of Self and not the other way round. Your Self is the smart one. Your mind is only the tool that you use to get things done. Without Self to oversee it, the mind functions on automatic pilot. It appears to know what it is doing but that is only an illusion.

"I am"—The universal healer

I have made some strong statements. Not the least passionate is that the loss of awareness of Self is the sole cause of human suffering. And awareness of Self ends suffering. So let's see if I can back those words up and put my awareness where my Self is.

Do experience one several more times. Your attention should be rewarded with a clearer, if not longer, glimpse of that gap between thoughts. It may have only lasted a second or two but it was there. Yes, it was there but what is *it*? Why, it is your Self! You were observing your Self.

Now, here comes the $64,000 question: When you were all alone with your Self, between thoughts, were there any feelings that were upsetting you? Do you remember any discomfort of any kind? There were none, were there? And, if you did a real good job observing the gap, you may also notice that you are feeling a little more peaceful. Go ahead, try it again. It will work every time. It is impossible to be angry, sad, worried, or guilty or in any way negative, at the same time you are fully aware of your inner Self. Impossible!

This is not simple misdirection. When you experience more "no-thinking" you will experience less discordant thoughts and feelings. Less discordant thoughts and feelings means clearer, friendlier thinking and a greater ability to solve problems. People who spend time with their Selves on a regular basis live longer, more dynamic lives than they would otherwise. And they cause fewer problems for the rest of us.

"Well," you ask, "how can I go through life not thinking? Wouldn't I just ramble around aimlessly and bump into things?"

Get ready for the incredible part. You can do both. You can be aware of your Self while you think and feel and work and raise a family. In fact, you will derive greater joy out of doing even the most mundane chores when you combine activity with awareness of the unsinkable Self. Awareness of your Self during activity is the fulfillment of your deepest desire. You see, you can have your cake and eat it too. But before we can get a firmer grip on this idea we need to do a little preliminary groundwork. I would like you to continue taking a minute every hour or so to stop your thinking. Notice how the regular experience of Self begins to change your life. If you are experiencing some sort of negativity remember to do experience one often. Don't use it to fight against negativity. That won't work. Just have the experience and note any changes. Don't get in the way, just observe. Your practice will also have the double benefit of making the material in the next couple of chapters more meaningful. Then you will be ready for more experience.

MAIN POINTS FOR CHAPTER ONE

Who Am I?

- Peace cannot be gained by effort.

- There is only one lesson to be learned, to become aware of your Self.

- When humans become aware of their true nature problems effortlessly dissolve.

- Happiness is part of the problem, not the cure.

- The symptom of Self awareness is inner peace.

- Self is beyond the senses and beyond thought but easily experienced.

- "Me" is the individual personality that has changed over your lifetime.

- It is impossible to be negative while you are fully aware of your inner Self.

- Awareness of Self is the fulfillment of your deepest desire.

CHAPTER 2
How To See With New Eyes

"With the concepts which now prove to be fundamental to our understanding of nature, the universe begins to look more like a great thought than like a great machine."

Sir James Jeans

The ghost of Newton

The way we presently express our lives is not working. Inner peace has become an apparition, the stuff of myths and fairy tales. The warning signs are all around us. We choose to sleepwalk past them with our eyes on the future. We are convinced that if we work hard, love our families and pay our taxes we will be rewarded with the things we desire. This brand of somnambulism is epidemic. A quick look around at the state of our affairs and the rest of the world should snap us out of this nightmare. Observation alone should clearly demonstrate that our common lives are not working.

Why is that? Simple, we are living a lie. We believe that if we keep pecking away at our problems, one beautiful and magical day we will wake up with all our problems solved. Is that your experience so far? Do you know anyone who is problem free? Have money, good health, charity or any other endeavor ever elevated an individual to the exalted status of "problem free?" No, it hasn't. Despite an overwhelming landslide of evidence to the contrary we continue to act as if we will someday be free of problems.

Have you heard the saying, "The more you know, the more you know you don't know"? Or how about this one, "When I solve one problem two more take its place"? What is hidden within these words is the realization that we cannot conquer our world through sheer brute force of intellect. It is the influence of Newtonian physics that encourages us to collect more data and apply it to the problem at hand. The idea is that if we finally amass enough information we will be the masters of our fate. That would mean the end of suffering. This approach works well for resolving well-defined challenges like a leaky pipe, a squeaky swing (either in the backyard or on the golf course), overeating or learning to speak Japanese. It cannot resolve the major conflicts that make up our lives.

It cannot because our lives are complicated beyond comprehension. There is no possible way we could know all that needs to be known. Just the simple act of holding this book and reading its contents takes the synaptic firing of trillions of nerves impulses every second. That just involves the physical activity of reading. Can you imagine what power of organization is needed to change those electrical impulses into comprehension, into usable knowledge? I can't. It is beyond what my mind can appreciate because it is beyond my mind. And now, we are getting to the heart of the problem.

Classical physics, based largely on the contributions of Sir Isaac Newton, has been the blueprint for the way we live our lives for more than 200 years. It addresses the world we know with our senses, the world of trees and sky, cars and buildings, jobs and family. But, there is more to our lives than we can see, taste or hear. There is the very big and the very small, the galaxies in the heavens and the dancing energies beyond the atom. These worlds have as much, and more, influence on us as do our jobs and our families. If we think that they do not have significant impact on the way we live, we are simply living with our heads in the sand.

When a tree falls in the woods...

Quantum physics explores life beyond our senses. Major findings in the last several years are astounding to the point of being mystical. One such finding will help us understand our problem with problems.

Quantum mechanics has shown us that when we observe an event we actually influence the outcome of that event. During the first semester of my freshman year in college I had an English 101 class that met three mornings a week at 8:00 AM. I loved English and hated mornings. One damp and cold November morning the clouds were gray cotton hanging just above the trees. The classroom was hot and just as cheerless as the weather. My second cup of coffee and I slid behind a desk in the last row. The young instructor, excited about his first teaching assignment, was far more enthusiastic than any English teacher had a right to be. Didn't he know what time it was? Without any introduction, he smiled his "I'm going to wake you up with this one" smile and asked, "When a tree falls in the woods, and there is no one to observe it, does it still make a noise?"

My first thought was, of course a falling tree makes a noise when no one is around. What a ridiculous question. And then, another thought elbowed its way in from the back row of my mind. "What if it didn't?" How would we know?

We might leave a tape recorder behind and that would answer the question once and for all. But, what if some intelligence, say the same force that made the forest, could sense the presence of a man-made device? What if that force could produce the very results that the men who left it behind would expect? That too seemed absurd. How could dawdling old Mother Nature outsmart man? After all, won't it be just a matter of time before we are in complete control our environment? We build roads and drive cars, manufacture malls and spend money, erect houses and control the climate inside them. We're pretty good at that. We'll get even better with time. Or do the forces of nature and the workings of the universe have other plans for us?

The original question, so casually shared by my instructor, took on a life of its own. He must have had a point to make pertaining to English 101 but I don't remember a thing he said after he asked that deceptively convoluted question. I guess he did wake me up, but not as he had intended. I barely remember leaving the class and walking outside. The crisp air slapped my cheek and I looked up into a cloudless blue sky.

Just a little bit of science

I heard that question for the first time almost 40 years ago. Back then, we thought we had most of the answers and that our scientific method would soon reveal all that was necessary for us to become the masters of our fate. And, as our own masters, we would be happy and finally at peace. Now, we see things differently.

Quantum mechanics' classic two-slit experiment demonstrates that just the act of observing an event changes the results. In spirit, the new science has answered the question my English teacher asked so long ago. We now know with absolute certainty that the event of a tree falling in the forest will be different if someone is there to watch it take place. Now hold onto your hats. The latest research is suggesting that any event is only a potential. That is, there are an infinite number of ways things can work out. A situation remains in seed form, and does not unfold, *until it is observed*!

Now don't get your knickers in a twist. It is not necessary that you have a working knowledge of quantum physics here. Fortunately, intellectual understanding is not a prerequisite to inner peace. I mention it only to offer you another perspective on your world. For, as you will soon see, a change in perspective is the first step in living a life free of suffering and full of meaning, fulfilling your deepest desire.

Two simple rules

A perceptual shift in the mind can often remove much confusion in your life. Let me offer two simple rules that will help your mind make a shift that can relieve much self-imposed suffering. Throughout my adult life, I have been guided by these two simple axioms of insight. These rules have afforded me both comfort and direction. The first one is "life is harmony." That is, there is always order in the universe, even when there appears to be none. The second dictum is this: "the world is not as I see it." It is impossible for me to know, feel or perceive everything for any given situation and therefore my comprehension has to be incomplete. For me, these simple aphorisms have had a profound influence on my personal evolution. If the world were not harmonious then I might accept suffering or limitation as being natural. If I felt that my view of the world was complete then I might feel that my position was the "correct" one. Whenever I became stuck or in a rut, I reminded myself that life is basically joyful and that my perception was not reflecting that fullness.

I soon began to see behind the scenes. Slowly these two simple rules persuaded me to loosen my grip and let life pass by like a meandering melody. Actually that makes for a good analogy. Music is enjoyed to its fullest when we let the melody flow through our consciousness like a river. If we try to hold onto even a single note we miss the synergy of the composition. Our lives, like music, should be free to flow. Holding onto people, ideas and things disrupts the flow and ruins the melody.

You and I are the same, and we are completely different. We bond through our sameness. Our differences add sweetness to our sameness. When these two opposites find balance, all things benefit. This has always been the formula for complete and prosperous living. I am writing to tell you this, not because I think that you don't know it, but because you may have forgotten it. I live by these two principles not because of some cumbersome philosophy, but because they come to me from my previous life as a child. They are the beacons of childhood before time was taught and space filled with the "necessary and practical" tools for successful living. If you should wish to explore the validity of these two simple rules, don't start by remembering what was forgotten. Start where you are right now, before memory or hope can take hold.

What you expect is what you get

We have a subtle and profound effect on everything and everyone around us. Everything is under our control, just not the way we think. We do make things happen but not by our actions. Change takes place simply by observing. And who said science is boring? Until this phenomenon was discovered we thought that we could observe life without altering it. Classical scientists taught us to be "objective observers." It turns out that there is no such thing. We can not exist without influencing every other thing in creation. This discovery has a very profound implication. What we think is overt control over an object or event is actually the illusion of control.

Here's how it works. According to quantum physics, before something is created it is a cloud of energy just waiting for someone (an observer) to give it direction. This energy takes form around our expectations. When we approach a problem we first observe it. As soon as we observe the problem the seeds for change are already beginning to sprout. Just the act of observing sets in motion the solution in the direction we expect. Now it is a bit more convoluted than this, which is why we don't always get what we expect. But still, this discovery has appreciable importance. It means that events move in the direction we expect. I guess that makes our expectations pretty important.

What is interesting is that almost all of us expect to have problems. Why shouldn't we? Our parents and their parents did. In fact, the whole collective human consciousness, reaching back beyond memory, seems to have expected to suffer and struggle. It is a cycle that has remained unbroken except by a few luminaries and gentle souls in every generation.

Extraordinary people

There are people whose expectations are different than most of ours. These are people who have made the transition to adulthood and not lost the innocence, joy and power of childhood. They are rare but perhaps you have been fortunate enough to personally known one of them. These exceptional people are content as they are where they are. They are more responsive to beauty. They are less driven by egocentric needs and more helpful and responsive to the needs of others. They are less fearful. They are creative, innovative and playful. They are loveable and have an impish sense of humor. You may find yourself being drawn to them and perhaps thinking, "This is a wonderful human being. If we could all be like her our world would be a safe and beautiful place."

Abraham Maslow calls these people "Transcenders." They make up a small percentage, possibly as little as one half of one percent, of the total human race. But they are there, and they are real. The question is, "Can we get what they have?"

The answer is "YES." We can fill our lives with peace, joy and love. We can eliminate fear, guilt, frustration and that underlying sense of unease that, like the sound of a noisy air conditioner during an unusually hot summer is always running in the background.

We are human beings and we are not finished. We are just emerging from our cocoon. Transcenders are the butterflies of our species. They show us what we are capable of becoming. And that is inspiring. But that is not enough.

Knowing that we are not complete is the first step to becoming whole. We feel it bubble up from deep inside when we are very quiet. It is a feeling of incompleteness, a sense that something is missing. One way we often try to drown out that uneasy feeling is by becoming busy, very busy. The more that feeling of emptiness tries to poke its meddlesome head into our conscious business the more we work to trample it under the two feet of work and worry. "I'm a workaholic," we hear a businessman say with pride. "I always have to be doing something. Sitting around is a waste of time," we hear a woman say about her life in general. These are unmistakable symptoms of emptiness. We have been infected by an insidious plague to which many have succumbed. The modern-day visionary Eckhart Tolle observed that unhappiness and fear spread more quickly than a virus.

Knowing there is a problem is the first step to fixing it. Knowing there are others who have overcome the same trials we face is encouraging. It is encouraging and it is a trap. For this is a solo journey unique to each one of us. Books, people and organizations are only signposts. They can only point in the direction that they feel is best for them. Your path to wholeness lies down a road only you can tread. In my mind I see an immense school of quick, silvery fish swimming in complete harmony. When the leader turns, all the fish turn with him. What a wonderful show of unity. But what if the leader is lost? What if he is headed toward the jaws of a ferocious predator?

Mirror vision

How do these people that Maslow calls Transcenders differ from us? That their perception of this world is different than the rest of humankind is obvious. Perception dictates expectation. Do they somehow tap into the world of quantum mechanics? Are they able to see the subtle workings of creation and realize that life, as it opens to our senses, is but a small part of the majesty and wholeness of creation? The answer is as plain as the nose on your face.

How plain is the nose on my face? Let's take a peek. From where I look out upon the world my nose is not very obvious at all. I have a singular view of it everywhere I go. I can close my right eye and see the blurry left side of my nose. I can repeat the process with the left eye, and that pretty much exhausts my possibilities.

When I enlist the aid of a mirror however, a whole new world opens up. Holding a mirror in front of my face I can see my nose very clearly. Moving the mirror around I can see both sides and the top of my nose clearly. I can even see into my nose when I hold the mirror below it. Imagine the possibilities.

I feel that Transcenders are able to have "mirror" vision. They are able to see life from more than one perspective. Indeed, there are no limits to the number of different angles from which they view the potential of any single event. This ability affords them a very curious and enviable position. They are capable of an infinite number of perspectives. What that means is that they effectively have no expectations. They observe and interact with the world as it is, not as they want it to be. The Transcenders individual mind has become one with those of the cosmic mind. They have relinquished their sense of individuality for one of universality.

To Transcenders life is an adventure. Knowing that the potential for any situation is infinite they do not try to interfere with the outcome. They do not try and impose their will for personal gain as the rest to us have learned to do. Transcenders are content to watch the beauty of creation unfold before them. The unifying force of the universe is beyond comprehension by the human mind. Our minds simply cannot know all of the possible combinations inherent in a single event. Forces from every direction and every level and of every kind are brought to bear on every event, every moment of every hour, day, year, millennium on into infinity. I have trouble remembering the combination to my post office box. I am not about to tackle the combination to creation.

Observation—A Full-time job

I don't have to. Creation takes care of itself. It appears that my *only* job is to observe that process unfolding. Does that mean that I sit around all day in a half-stupor as the world passes by my window? No. Maslow found that Transcenders are dynamic, creative and productive. Observing is a kind of letting go. It is awareness that there are infinite ways in which any single situation can unfold. Observing allows it to unfold without interference. When I let creation take care of itself the world is always new. One sure sign that you are trying to control things for your own personal gain is boredom. That's right, if you get bored it is because things are not going the way you are forcing them to go. Life loses its newness, becomes stale and uninteresting and you become bored. A child doesn't get board until she learns to set goals and get upset when she doesn't achieve them. Until then, a pot and a spoon will inspire her for hours.

While I am observing I am also doing. But get the order straight: Observe the Self and then perform an action. Remember: Be then do. Doing is a natural result of observing. It is not a natural result of planning. Just like thoughts don't come from other thoughts. They come from Self. There is nothing more damaging to our life's energy than to follow a plan that is working against itself. If you want to see how destructive that habit has become, then take a second to reflect on how we humans are killing the earth. This is not a real smart move. We have been likened to a cancer on the face of Mother Earth. When she breathes her last breath we will perish along with her. It is impossible for Transcenders to be destructive to themselves, others or their environment. That is because they are constantly observing what is and then doing what needs to be done.

Death is life

There is order in the universe, a kind of intelligent energy that appears to know what is going on everywhere at once. Quantum mechanics has many names for this universal order, including implicate order, un-manifest, sub-manifest, and vacuum state. When this energy/order goes to work all we need do is get out of the way and watch. When I was a student in Chiropractic College I was taught that the power that made the body heals the body. As chiropractic physicians we were taught to "find it, fix it and leave it alone." This philosophy offers deep insight into how universal order manifests and how observing works.

When you cut your finger, how hard is it to get the cut to heal? Do you have to coax it along, encourage it, pray for it or bribe it to heal? You need do nothing. The power that made the body heals the body. You may do some things to enhance the healing such as clean the cut and put a band-aid on it. But the healing takes place because universal energy/order is being expressed as life in your body. Clean and bandage the cut on a cadaver and see how much healing takes place.

With death we observe a different energy/order. This is the order of destruction. This is also an expression of universal order. It is not bad. It is just different.

Without destruction we would be in a real pickle. Death is a natural part of life and must be allowed to unfold for life to unfold. When a bud on the branch of a cherry tree opens we rejoice in its beauty. When the blossom begins to wither and die we rejoice again for the fruit of the cherry tree will soon burden the branches. When the fruit rots and falls to the ground with seed we rejoice again. A new tree will be born and also die. There is no thing, idea or event that dwells outside this cosmic cycle. Even the desire to overcome death will die. When the desire to overcome death does finally die there is a void vacated by the will. In that void, beyond the desire to live, dwells the progenitor of the Self, that which was never born and will never die.

If this sounds all too cryptic or mystical do not carelessly toss this thinking aside. Even the language of science today sounds strangely enigmatic and obscure. But it only seems that way to the concept-bound mind. What the mind cannot understand can be experienced simply and in a single moment. Soon you will learn to step outside your mind and become a pure observer. A simple change of perspective and your life will change forever and for better.

MAIN POINTS FOR CHAPTER TWO

How To See With New Eyes

- We approach problems as if we will someday be free of them.

- We cannot conquer our world through sheer brute force of intellect.

- The two simple rules that shift perception and remove suffering are: 1) there is always order in the universe; 2) the world is not as I see it.

- What we think is overt control over an object or event is actually the illusion of control.

- Transcenders have relinquished their sense of individuality for one of universality.

- Boredom is a sure sign that you are trying to control life for personal gain.

- Performing an action is a natural result of observing. It is not the result of planning.

- Death is a natural part of life and must be allowed to unfold for life to unfold.

CHAPTER 3
How The Mind Works

"The mind must learn that beyond the moving mind there is the background of awareness, which does not change."
Nisargadatta Maharaj

Thinking

The unattended mind has caused a world of grief. It will be of great value for us to take a quick look at the mechanics of the distracted mind.

If you want to perform some action, say, get out of your chair, walk across the room and turn on the light, what must first happen in your mind? Right, you must first have a thought before you can carry out an action. The thought may be conscious or subconscious but either way it is thought. Thought also controls our senses. Just the action of flipping the light switch takes remarkable coordination between mind and body. Your hand must be guided to the switch by sight. Your mind makes continual adjustments in the position of your hand as it approaches the switch. It feels the switch and hears the familiar click as it snaps on. Your eyes tell you that your efforts have been successful and your life is a little brighter as a result. This simple feat is infinitely more complicated than I have outlined here. But the basics are accurate and certainly complete enough for our purposes.

I would like to take a moment to explain the difference between brain and mind. At least, how I will use those words in this book. Some sources use them interchangeably. Some say the brain creates the mind and others hold that the mind creates the brain. It would be counterproductive for us to join in this long-standing debate. The brain is a physical structure subject to physical laws. The mind, obviously, belongs in the mental model. And, as we shall see, the mind includes thinking, feeling, memory and a few other goodies soon to be unveiled.

Feeling

Now, we've just explored how thinking is necessary for action to take place. Thinking influences action. But, what influences our thinking? Right again! Feeling influences thinking.

Do you have your doubts? You probably will if you consider yourself objective in your approach to life. The scientific thinker who feels he can remove himself from outside influences, including emotion, and be completely objective is an endangered species. Quantum mechanics has clearly proven that there is no such thing as an objective observer. The purely logical, analytical and objective point of view is an illusion.

On the most fundamental level of life there are only waves. Thoughts are waves and feelings are a different kind of waves.

Feeling influences thinking. If you are angry with a friend you will have angry thoughts about them. The anger acts as an engine adding power to your thoughts. You may even find yourself thinking in ways that would, at a less emotional time, seem ridiculous. A suspicious lover will see infidelity where none exists. An angry child may wish her parents dead. Feelings can drastically distort our thinking and completely change our perception of reality. Feelings are also affected by thinking. But of the two, feelings are subtler and immensely more powerful.

Security

What influences feeling? What determines if a feeling is uplifting and loving or destructive or hurtful? Simply put, our feelings are influenced by how secure we believe we are. Our security is based on how safe we perceive our circumstance.

Let's suppose that you have worked for a company for 18 years. Like many companies, it is experiencing a host of problems and one of the corrective measures it has enlisted is downsizing. In your office several people have already been let go, some of them senior to you. There are strong rumors that your whole department will be eliminated.

You have been an exemplary employee. You have been loyal, energetic and only missed work 17 times in 18 years. You are a team player and have saved the company thousands of dollars during your tenure by helping to streamline office procedures.

It is Friday afternoon, the chosen time of execution. When you returned from lunch, there on your desk was a pink office memo asking you to immediately report to your boss' office. Your mind is a whirlwind of thoughts and emotions, all malicious. You are feeling betrayed. You are angry, defensive and afraid.

You are swept away by a flood of thoughts, which go something like this. "I've given this company the best years of my life. They never appreciated my or my work or me. Sure my boss has been nice but I never trusted him. And what's with that squirrelly growth on his upper lip he calls a mustache? He probably drinks too much and kicks the dog. God, I hate this company."

On the way to the boss' office you start to notice that your stomach is tied in knots, your palms are sweating and your legs are weak. These are physical symptoms brought on by agitated thoughts bubbling in a stew of volcanic emotions.

When you walk into the office there sits your boss behind his expensive desk with several golf clubs leaning against the wall. He begins to speak, "As you know the company has been cutting back in all departments. Soon your department will be completely eliminated.

"I knew it." you hiss under your breath, "My world is over."

He continues, "You are one of our most valued employees. You have been a great asset and your loyalty has been noted and greatly appreciated. A new department is being formed to help our company make this transition and we would like you to manage it for us. While your hours will remain the same we would like to offer you a significant rise in salary. What do you say?"

In an instant, you are transformed. You now love your company. You love your job and you even love your boss' squirrelly mustache. You are convinced that he is a saint and his dog is lucky to have him. All of your unpleasant bodily symptoms have been replaced by the physical equivalent of joy. You are on top of the world.

So, what just happened? How were you able to ascend from the depths of distress to the extremes of ecstasy in a single heartbeat? Of course, you experienced a shift from being very insecure to being very secure. The perceptual shift from insecure to secure clearly impacted your feelings, which influenced your thinking and even your physiology. This example gives a good opportunity to see how the mind works to make us happy, anxious, guilty, light-hearted or angry. When it comes right down to it we are really at the mercy of how secure we feel at any time, in any situation. And this exposes what I feel to be the heart of suffering for us all. If we go no further than this point we will continue to be at the mercy of the mind. The next step is to find the single force that influences our sense of security and ultimately our whole mind, our body and in the end our environment.

If we can find out what supports our security then maybe we will discover how to be more secure, or even completely secure. We all know individuals who appear calm and supportive in the midst of the most traumatic events. There are many examples of people who lived inner lives of peace and joy despite enduring great personal hardships, Mahatma Gandhi, Mother Teresa, Albert Schweitzer to name a few. The great religions of the world have added many more. If one human can do it then we all have the potential. After all, it was Christ who told us, "All these things you can do, and more."

MAIN POINTS FOR CHAPTER THREE

How The Mind Works

- Thought precedes action.

- Thought directs the senses to gather feedback in preparation for further action.

- Feeling influences thinking.

- Feelings are also affected by thinking. But of the two, feelings are subtler and immensely more powerful motivators.

- Security influences feeling.

CHAPTER 4
How Time Works

*"When a man sits with a pretty girl for an hour, it seems like a
minute. But let him sit on a hot stove for a minute—and it's longer
than any hour. That's relativity."*

Albert Einstein

Time is not on my side

As it turns out, our security is intimately tied to how we view time. And how we
view time depends on how well we know Self. When we are conscious of Self we
are secure. When we are not conscious of Self we become insecure and our feelings, thoughts and actions reflect that insecurity.

I know of three kinds of time. There is Cosmological time. That clock started
with the Big Bang. It has taken time for the universe to expand to this point. That
is what Cosmological time measures.

Then there is Thermodynamic time. It takes time for things, cups, people, and
planets to wear out and break down into the atoms that made them. Thermodynamic time measures the breakdown of things.

The first two kinds of time are more objective ways to measure the material
world. Cosmological and Thermodynamic time operate outside the mind.

The third kind of time is psychological time. It measures what goes on inside
your mind. Psychological time is subjective and inaccurate. In fact, it really can't
be relied on to measure much of anything outside the mind. Psychological time is
an illusion and it is the cause of all the problems facing human kind.

Before you get your knickers in a twist, let's take a few minutes to understand
how psychological time works.

Psychological time is an illusion. (When I use the word "time" by itself I am
referring to psychological time. The objective measure of time I will call "real"
time, outside time or clock time.) We mistakenly think that time has always been
there and that we just learned about it at some point in our life. Your mind actu-

38

ally invented time. It wasn't always there.

Watch a young child at play. There is no time in his world. Every parent knows the frustration of trying to dress, feed and generally motivate a timeless child. Their inner clock is set to "now." As outside time passes and we grow from children to adults, our mind constructs an inner, psychological clock. Eventually, "now" is overwhelmed by a torrent of thoughts about past and future.

Popcorn, pop and pure consciousness

I love to go to the movies. For a couple of hours I become completely engrossed in the obvious illusion unfolding on the screen. When I step into that theatre I leave my everyday life behind. Although the movie is only a flickering of light and shadow, it represents the greater illusion we call "real life" waiting for us just outside the theatre doors.

The illusion of movement is created in our minds when thought oscillates between past and future. Thoughts of future and past construct a mental bridge crossing over the ever-present now. It is like watching a movie. Movie film is a long strip of individual pictures or frames. In a single second 24 still frames flash on the screen. This is faster than our brains can individually process and so it looks like the still pictures are in motion. That is pretty amazing. We see motion where there is none. That is the illusion that a movie produces.

Likewise, time is the illusion that the mind produces. Individual thoughts are like the individual frames of movie film. Individual thoughts occur so quickly they appear to be moving. That illusion of motion is what we call time.

When we think about future events we are moving forward in time. When we visit our memories we are moving back in time. All this movement takes place in the mind. It exists nowhere else in this universe but in your mind. Your time, your future and your past, is not shared by anyone else.

The movie projector works on a simple principle. A bright, white light shines through the film and creates a picture on the screen in the front of the theatre. The movement of the film, frame by frame through the light, creates the illusion of movement on the screen. As the audience, we sit contentedly watching the drama of the actors unfold, forgetting that they are merely light and shadow created by a bright light shinning through film at the back of the theatre. We cry and we laugh as if the illusion were real.

Our life is just like that movie. It unfolds thought-by-thought, minute-by-minute, year-by-year. We, the audience, get completely absorbed in the drama of our own movie. We worry over the bills, love the new house, watch the children grow up and contemplate our own death. Like a movie, our lives are an illusion, a play of light and shadow. Don't get me wrong. Our lives exist, but not the way we think they do. This mistaken identity causes an overwhelming suffering that only deepens with each generation.

What time is it?—NOW!

What is this mistaken identity? Simply, that time exists. We think that our past and our future exist. There is usually a lot of resistance to the idea that the past and future do not exist. That is because we have never really thought about it. But think about it we must if we are ever going to find lasting peace.

Let me ask you a question. Did you ever have an experience that did not happen now? You may have a memory of an experience but that is only a memory, a present thought about the past. An event can only happen in the present. The past is gone. It does not exist. The future is not here. It will never get here. It can't, it's the future. So if the past doesn't exist and the future doesn't exist, that leaves us with only...NOW. And really, now only exists because we recognize future and past. When future and past die to the mind, now becomes what is. There can only be a now if you have a not-now. But let's look more closely at the phenomenon of time as reflected in the mind.

"Well, sure," you say, "every experience I've ever had happened before now." It is true, you have a memory of an experience and the memory says that it happened in the past. But, a memory is a thought. And you are thinking that thought now. Rent a video, take it home and watch it on your TV. During the movie push the pause button on the remote control. What you see is a single frame frozen on your screen. If you had a remote control for your mental movies and you pushed the pause button you would see a single thought. That is the thought you are having now. There is only now. There never has been, nor will there ever be, a time that is not now.

Does this seem a little confusing? Do you feel that what you have just read almost feels right but you can't quite make sense of it? You may even feel an almost imperceptible stirring deep inside as if some part of you that has been asleep is starting to awaken? There is a good reason for this. We have given the mind a puzzle that it cannot solve. This is probably not the first time the mind has been at a loss for thoughts. The elation of new love or a brilliant sunset is timeless and beyond the mind. What is beyond the mind cannot be understood by the mind. It can't get there from here. To solve the puzzle we must step out of the mind. We must go beyond psychological time.

Fortunately, you already know how to do that. Remember when you asked, "Where will my next thought come from?" Remember the gap that was created when your thoughts stopped? You were observing, not thinking. You experienced no mind. In other words, you went beyond your mind.

When you go beyond the mind you stop time. That is because the mind created time. When you stop time you are free of the illusion of past and future. When you are free of past and future you put an end to suffering.

What a wonderful discovery you are

Let's modernize the famous analogy of Plato's Cave and take our movie analogy a little further at the same time. Let's say that you were born and raised in the movie theatre. The movie played continuously with no break. If a happy movie was playing, you were happy. If it was a sad movie, you cried. Your whole world revolved around watching the places, actors and events come and go. To you they were not the play of light and dark on a screen, they were real.

Then let's say one day you inadvertently found a switch right by your hand. When you flipped the switch the film stopped. Now, only the blank screen was illuminated and you discovered something quite interesting. You realized that the blank screen had always been there. If it hadn't been there you would not have been able to see the pictures.

During this period of "no movie" you were bathed in the pure, white light reflecting from the screen. You did not have the distraction of the film on the screen so you became acutely aware of your own body and actions. The blank screen did not divert your mind from who you really are. What a wondrous discovery you were.

The secret of your life has been revealed. You are not the movie. You are separate from it. You are real. The movie is illusion. You will never be the same. Then you flip the switch on and the movie starts again. But this time you are aware that you are separate from the film. You no longer believe you are in the movie. With the dawning of this knowledge your fears and worries vanish like the illusions they are. Now, the motion picture is there for your entertainment You passionately enjoy the unfolding drama on the screen with amused detachment. After all, you are sitting safely in your seat. With awareness of the screen comes awareness of the Self.

MAIN POINTS FOR CHAPTER FOUR

How Time Works

- Our security is intimately tied to how we view time. And how we view time depends on how conscious we are of our Self.

- Psychological time is subjective and conditional.

- Psychological time is the cause of all the problems facing humankind.

- Psychological time is the illusion of motion.

- The mind set firmly on the present is at rest.

- Your time is only known by you. No one else can share your sense of time. No one can share the illusion that you know as your life.

- Our future and our past do not exist except right now, in the mind.

- Awareness of Self breaks the illusion of time.

- When you are Self-aware and free of time you are free of suffering.

CHAPTER 5

Innerthink

"Use your own light and return to the source of light. This is called practicing eternity."

Tao Te Ching

Five levels of consciousness

I would like to ask you a simple question, the answer to which could change your life forever. Put the book in your lap for a few minutes, think it through thoroughly, and then continue reading. Here is the question: "What is your most valuable possession? What is most vital in your life?"

What did you come up with? Health? Mind? Family? Job? Ice cream? A human being's most vital possession is his/her conscious awareness. Other words that mean the same thing are consciousness, wakefulness, alertness or attention. If we are not conscious, then what meaning is there to life? If we are unaware then life does not exist.

Now, let me ask you another question: "What is the most vital kind of conscious awareness?" Take a few moments to think it over. Close your eyes, if you can, and play with the possibilities.

How did you do? If you said "Self" awareness you hit the jackpot. What is Self-awareness? Simply put, it is awareness of what you are underneath all the trappings of life. Yes, you are a human. You are a man or woman. You may be a child or an adult, a doctor, lawyer or Indian chief. But, these are all categories that change with the passage of clock time. They are things you call yourself while identifying with a group or class, ideal or philosophy. They are inventions of the mind. And we already know we are not our minds.

Part of the Science of Creative Intelligence as taught by Maharishi Mahesh Yogi included a very clear understanding of different levels of conscious awareness. I would like to introduce you to the basic concepts and I have adapted some of the terms to better suit our particular needs. There are five basic levels of consciousness awareness. There is the waking state of consciousness, the dreaming state, sleeping state, pure consciousness and, the fifth state I call innerthink. Each state of conscious awareness is distinct. With each one the mental and physical functions are uniquely different.

When awake our minds are active and our bodies are active. When we are in deep, dreamless sleep, our minds and bodies are deeply at rest. When we dream our minds and bodies are not as quiet as deep sleep but more quiet than when we are awake. The waking state is the one we are most familiar with and has many variations or grades of consciousness awareness. You can be tired, wide-awake, confused, drunk, and so on. Waking, dreaming and deep sleep are the common experience of all humans.

The fourth kind of consciousness awareness is pure consciousness. That is the awareness of the gap between thinking. It is the first tender appreciation of Self-awareness. There is nothing mystical about pure consciousness. When you want to experience the sleep state you just lie down and wait. Healthy people fall asleep effortlessly. Dreaming naturally flows from deep sleep. The experiences of waking, dreaming and deep sleep are natural and so is the experience of Self. When you asked yourself, "Where will my next thought come from?" you spontaneously experienced a gap in your thinking. You were experiencing your pure Self, the pure "You" before you take on all the roles, responsibilities, hopes, plans, worries, guilt, or fear you have come to identify as your life. Unfortunately, awareness of the Self has become a rare occurrence. When Self-awareness is lost, harmony is lost and life is thrown out of balance.

What innerthink is and how it works

The fifth state is innerthink. It is also natural and easy to experience. Technically, it is not a level of consciousness awareness. It is the combination of the state of Self-awareness with the waking state, and even sleeping and dreaming. When we are innerthinking, harmony and balance are regained in our lives.

When you flipped the switch that turned off the movie you saw, for the first time, the screen that supported the moving pictures. The I Am is like that screen. It supports the mental activity of the mind. Without it your mind would not exist as a movie could not exist without the screen. If we don't switch off thinking we cannot know what we truly are. And knowing our essential nature is vital if we are to live life with beauty, boldness and grace.

When we do discover I Am, our lives change in a most remarkable way. Again, let us refer back to the movie theater analogy. When we switched the movie off, two remarkable things happened. First, we became aware that we were not the movie we were watching. We were separate from that illusory action. We are whole by ourselves and did not need the drama displayed on the screen to feel alive.

Second, when the movie started again we maintained our newfound awareness. We did not loose our Self in the play and display of light and shadow on the screen. This is a critical change in our perspective and one worthy of much closer scrutiny.

This new perception gives us a perspective that frees us from the illusion that we are just the mind. This is innerthinking.

Why is this so important? Experiencing your Self as different from your mind frees you from identification with something that is not you. Or, more accurately it is only a part of you. If you think that you are your mind you only live part of your life. That would be like owning a mansion and living your whole life in just one room. When you become aware that you are more than your mind you open the door to living in every room of your life.

Innerthinking begins at the level of I Am, beyond thoughts. You are able to hold the awareness that I Am not thought at the same time you start having thoughts again. Once you get used to the idea and experience that you are beyond thought then you can add thinking, feeling and even the activity of daily living without creating further disharmony in your life. Innerthinking creates unshakable security. It nurtures deep and unremitting Stillness. Slowly, you will realize that thoughts are projected on the screen of I Am. The value of innerthinking is the same as knowing that you are not the movie. *Inner peace comes from innerthinking.* As stress melts away you are free to watch with intrigue the unfolding of the movie of "me."

You will enjoy a sense of unlimited joy and unshakable peace. You will see the world through new eyes, the eyes of a child filled with wonder. What you used to consider boring or a waste of your time will be fresh and alive. You will lose that anxious feeling that you should be somewhere else or should be doing something constructive. You will be at home no matter where you are.

I was recently invited to the office of an editor of a magazine to review several articles I had written. He told me that the building was under repair and to please excuse the clutter. When I arrived for my appointment he was still busy with other business and asked me to wait. The only place to wait was outside. It was in the low 90's. I found a large bush and if I stood just right I was completely in the shade. I stood still, facing the traffic 30 feet away. I stood there for a half hour not moving. I observed the traffic noises and the faces in passing cars. My eyes tracked a crow across the sky above the city. I heard its faint caw before it was crushed beneath the noise of moaning tires on hot pavement. I felt the heavy hand of heat squeezing me like a sponge. Rivulets of sweat trickled down my forehead, chest and back. I was uncomfortable and I was in bliss. I was innerthinking.

Innerthinking will free you from fear, guilt, boredom and even much physical pain. I don't mean that you will lack emotion or enthusiasm. On the contrary, you will become more vibrant, more interactive, more loving and less stressed, agitated and irritable. Your friends and family will notice an inner strength that surrounds you and makes them feel at ease when you are with them. Seemingly out of nowhere, great opportunities will offer themselves to you.

You will have goals and aspirations but they will not be a source of anxiety and stress. The primary goal to "Know Thy Self" will have already been realized. You will fulfill your relative goals with a detached air of ease. And, you will not feel empty after completing a major goal or feel the need to quickly create another project to fill the emptiness left by the first. Absolutely, the most vital of human experiences is innerthinking. Everything after that is window dressing. Everything after that is joy.

Don't mind the mind

If you have been having a difficult time following along, here is the reason why. You have been using your mind to "understand" what is being said. We have been discussing the Self, the I Am. And as we have already seen, I Am is beyond the mind. It is bigger than the mind and can never completely be understood by the mind.

There are two good reasons for this approach to innerthinking. First, I want you to become aware of the limitations of your mind. It is common to think that our minds can solve any of the problems that confront us today. This is a trick. The mind is actually creating more problems than it solves. The way we approach life is insane. We are a cancer that will kill its host and succumb to our own reckless behavior. At least at that time all our problems will be solved.

David Bohm, a quantum mechanical theorist and considered by Einstein to be his intellectual son, tells us that our minds are the problem. They are not complete by themselves. He points out that thinking has created disharmony and to try and use thinking to fix it is pure lunacy. That is like trying to pick up a chair while you are sitting in it. You must step outside the framework of the mind in order to fix it. Innerthinking is the experience outside the mind.

Second, I wanted to acquaint you with the tools to experience "no mind." I am offering you the opportunity to go beyond your mind and begin living life fully and with purpose. I am offering you the chance to stop being part of the problem and be the solution.

Whether you understand the mechanics of living a harmonious life is not important. Ultimately, a harmonious life is beyond understanding. Living that life on the other hand, is vitally important and starts with the experience of I Am. It is so simple as to be laughable and yet we repeatedly choose to turn away from our Self in favor of short-term gains and instant gratification.

Space—The final frontier

Space is born simultaneously with creation. The idea of space, like the idea of time, begins in the mind. If there were no things then there would be no space. It would be the unbounded Self. The Self is space-less, an unbounded sea of awareness. When there is no time and no space there is only I Am. Let's do another exercise. This one comes from Douglas Harding in his book, "Look for Yourself."

Experience Two
Finding Unbounded Space

Hold both of your hands out in front of you at arms length about 12 inches apart. Keep your palms facing each other about a foot apart. Focus on the space that is between your hands. Now, slowly bring your hands in toward your face. Keep your attention not on your hands, but the space between your hands. Then, let your hands pass by your eyes and right by the sides of your head while continuing to be aware of the space.

What happened? What did you feel as your hands disappeared and the space became unbounded? When the limited space between the hands disappeared it was replaced by unlimited space. Perform this exercise several more times slowly, being very much aware of the space between your palms, and how you feel when that space is no longer defined by your hands.

Along with this shift in perception comes a feeling of expansion or wholeness that cannot be analyzed by the mind. When you experience unbounded space it is always accompanied with a stillness of mind, the result of the direct perception of "I Am space-less." This stillness is peaceful, even joyful. You may have found yourself smiling or feeling a sense of wonder when your insight shifted from limited to unlimited. It doesn't make sense to the mind but nevertheless the shift in your perception was real. When you did you were completely secure in your Self, without fear, concern or worry. This expanded vision is the corner stone of your renaissance.

Here is what I mean. This simple exercise opened your vision to the unbounded Self by momentarily eliminating things. It took you from what you look at to what you are. All of a sudden you became aware of the space surrounding things, then unbounded space that is everywhere. Your mind did not wrap around a model of infinite space. The mind is not made to do that. You were just aware that without things, unbounded space goes on without end. You didn't have to try to see it, work it out on a computer or intellectually debate it. Those activities are all functions of the mind, which cannot "get it." In fact, all mental activity stopped for that instant and you were left all alone with your Self.

Make time for space

Let's play some more with this idea that I Am is in the gap between thoughts. The complete stoppage of time and the total expansion of space is I Am. There is nothing mystical about it. That is it! If you have read that it takes many years of arduous study and sacrifice to know thy Self, then you have just proven otherwise. If you have heard that it is hard to clear the mind of thought, then you now know differently. Experiencing that you are I Am is the simplest thing we can achieve. We have had it backward all this time.

We have a fragmented worldview. The mind is a thing. It relates to other things. But we have become convinced that the mind is in control. From that platform we move out into the world to appease the mind's insatiable hunger for more. To the mind, more is better, more money, more love, more power, more…What it really wants is the most. The most is I Am, the unbounded, infinite Self. When the mind finds I Am it stops and rests. It has fulfilled its prime directive, to find the most. You cannot get more than your Self.

It does not get confusing until the mind jumps in again and starts analyzing, organizing and generally trying to fit the unbounded nature of I Am into a neat little box. The mind likes to feel that once it defines something, it owns that thing. Maybe you know people who are acting on this overt tendency of the mind to dominate over things. They tend to state their opinion as if it were fact. They are very sure they are right and you will rarely hear them say,"I don't know." In their mind, they can know anything. This mind gets frustrated with the experience of Self as it cannot be owned by defining it. Once it surrenders to this fact, knowing the Self becomes easy and effortless.

So we can throw out the idea that to know thy Self is hard. Why then, have so few of us made it to the big time? There are a few saints and saint-like people in every generation. They are lighthouses, shining examples of what we can be. They all expound the same basic truths. And yet, 99.9% of us continue to suffer despite their guidance.

There is an old saying that comes out of ancient India, "When the wise man points at the moon, the unwise look at his finger." The wise man is one who knows the Self, who knows that he is I Am. The unwise are in a trance. The good news is that anyone can awaken from this identity crisis and join the wise for an evening of moon watching. Anyone means you. Do it now!

The first crack in the wall of suffering

We have identified the gap in thoughts as unbounded Self. But what does that mean in regards to our own peace and joy? Sure, during that brief experience of the gap I am not suffering, I feel no pain. I am not angry, hungry or running through my grocery list. I just Am. So what?

Even though you have just eliminated suffering, albeit for a briefest of moments, you may still feel the need to expand it. This is a symptom of mind's need to control. Perhaps you are wondering how you can bottle and market the gap. This is very natural in the beginning. These brief moments of freedom are quickly covered over by years of mental plaque. In other words, the mind quickly regains control and discomfort, defensiveness and frustration start working their way back into your consciousness.

Is this gap enough? Are you to settle for this limited and rather bland experience of Universality? What seems more like a parlor game than the gateway to universal peace is actually the first crack in the wall of suffering. It should at least be enough to inspire you to take a closer look at this simple but profound state. But if it is not, don't worry. There is more. Well, really not more. How can you get more than the most? It is your perception, your refined awareness that allows you to go beyond the mind and just be with your Self. Perception can become increasingly refined. You can learn to appreciate your Self on more and more refined levels. This leads your life in the direction of greater and greater peace, joy and love. Your mission, should you accept it, would be to continue to refine your perception and enjoy ever more subtle and beautiful levels of awareness. Come along with me and that is precisely what we will do.

Spaced out—In a good way

Can I Am observe I Am? Of course it can. Remember, I Am is everywhere. Then, who is I Am? Why, it is capital You, the Self.

I don't mean the material/mental small you with your thoughts, and feelings, a body and a job. I mean the You that is beyond all that. You are the Self, the I Am, pure awareness and universal presence. Are you beginning to get a hint as to how incredible You are?

When you entered the gap, You were still conscious. But there were no thoughts to be aware of. You were aware of no movement, no time. There was only You observing You, Self observing Self. When space expanded to infinity as your hands slipped beyond your eyes, you momentarily observed unbounded space. Space-less is also Self!

Your mind probably balked at the idea that you could be space. After all, that is *my* mind making *my* body move. But ask yourself, "Who is making the body and mind work?" You are aware that they exist, aren't you? But who is aware? What is awareness?

You are awareness and awareness is unbounded. The pinch is, when You focus on thinking and doing you habitually focus on the forms and forget their time-less/space-less roots. You forget that you are awareness and begin thinking that you are your mind and body.

When you are aware of just your Self, you are purely awake, aware and present. When you feel your own pure presence in this way you are free from the forms of thinking and feeling, body and outside world. When you are observing pure awareness, you are not thinking. You are just aware! Your existence comes from beyond the mind. Now, how amazing can that be?

It is only when you are caught up in the trials and traumas of day-to-day living that you forget who I Am is. You become like the man who did not know the movie screen existed and identified his life with the movie. The symptom of this misidentification is suffering. Just take a quick look around you. Do you think we are a species that is conscious of pure awareness? We have been told that what separates us from animals is that we are self-aware. Well, there is self-awareness and there is Self-awareness. Our self-awareness is awareness of "me." the little needs that define our damaging desires. It is precisely this "me" awareness that encourages our animal-like, destructive nature to surface. It is our Self-awareness, on the other hand, that frees us from the space/time bound mind that has caused the sorrow and suffering that we have come to associate with man. The good news is, you can change all that anytime you like.

Now, here is a biggie. When your hands disappeared past the sides of your head and the space that was between your palms expanded to infinity, did the things around you disappear? Did the wall, or desk or skyline in the background dissolve into unbounded space? Of course they didn't. Then, what did happen?

The moment your hands disappeared, your awareness expanded beyond the space bound between them. Bound space became unbounded. While you were having that flash of insight the objects in the room remained, but they were of *secondary* importance. You the observer was observing unbounded space and the environment was still there in the background. The objects were in their little spaces but your awareness was everywhere. Being aware of unbounded space means your awareness is unbounded. How much more exciting can this get? Or, as I like to say, "The key to abolishing suffering is in the palm of your hand." (Although I may suffer at the hands of my readers for that one.)

Innerthinking

Let's look at it another way. When you stop your thinking by paying close attention to where thoughts come from, You the observer is watching You the timeless space where thoughts used to be. And when thoughts start up again You, the observer, is still there. Only now you are observing thoughts where space used to be. This is Innerthinking. Innerthinking is observing your thoughts, emotions, eating, working, etc. while continuing to be aware that you are doing these things. First, you stopped thinking and then you realized that you were observing no thinking. Then You were there to watch when thinking started up again. At that point You continued to observe the thoughts. This demonstrated that You are separate from your thoughts. It was only after some time that you forgot your Self and the mind went back on autopilot. This is called autothink, the opposite of Innerthink.

This is so simple that we tend to dismiss the whole process as having no inherent value. Don't make that mistake! This key opens the gates to heaven. Just because it is easy don't toss it aside as worthless. Give it a chance and you will be rewarded beyond your wildest dreams.

Pennies from heaven

The first experiences of innerthinking are infinitesimally small doses of heaven. They are so small that they are sandwiched between big chunks of autothinking. It is the mind that is in control most of the time and it is telling you (remember you are not your mind) that this little blip on your radarscope of peace and joy is not worth concerning yourself with. But it is.

These little blips of peace start adding up. They are pennies in a kind of cosmic piggybank. These "innerthink" pennies accumulate very quickly, allowing a greater role for peace in daily life. That's all there is to it. Keep adding innerthink pennies and soon you will be living off of the interest alone. This is what we call momentum.

The good news—no, the great news—is that you can stop being run by your mind anytime you want. Do it now. Pay attention to your thoughts. Are you observing them? There you did it again. You are innerthinking. You, the observer, are like the parent and your mind is like a naughty child. If you don't watch it closely it will get into all kinds of mischief.

It is only a small step from watching your thinking to watching your actions, and the actions of others. How do you do that? Just pay attention. Flip off the autopilot and pay attention. Wake up and smell the roses, literally. Become a curious observer. Don't just look at the clouds, observe the clouds. See them as if you had never seen clouds before. Feel the bark, smell the air, taste the toothpaste.

Can it be that simple? The mind doesn't want you to think so. It will try and talk you out of it. Fortunately You are not your mind. You have the big picture. You are the big picture. The big picture is at peace with Itself. When you remove the blinders you experience a wholeness that brings with it inner peace. Yes, it is just that simple.

In the beginning, you may find your thoughts rushing back in. A second or two of stillness or peace and then thoughts fill the void like a flock of frightened birds scattering into the sky. After experiencing the gap your mind may produce thoughts something like these, "What was that? It was nothing. Nothing has no value. It was nice, though. I didn't hear angels singing, no fireworks. Maybe this is just a big hoax. I wonder if I have spinach in my teeth. Where is the cheese dip?" Thoughts lead you further and further away from the stillness that is You. It may be hours, or even days before your realize the trick your mind played on you. Thousands of thoughts pound like heavy rain on a tin roof drumming you back to sleep.

MAIN POINTS FOR CHAPTER FIVE

Innerthink

- Awareness is our most vital possession.

- With each state of awareness the mind and body functions are uniquely different.

- Innerthinking frees us from the illusion that we are just the mind, and therefore frees us from suffering.

- Inner peace comes from innerthinking.

- Innerthinking allows you to step outside the broken mind while it mends.

- The idea of space, like the idea of time, begins in the mind.

- Unbounded time and space is peace.

- Autothinking is when you are not aware of Self while you are thinking or acting. It is the opposite of innerthinking.

- Each time you innerthink you strengthen awareness of Self.

CHAPTER 6
How To Fix The Future

"Many eyes go through the meadow, but few see
the flowers in it."

Ralph Waldo Emerson

How to overcome anxiety

Is your mind always where you aren't? Do you forget what you just did because your mind was thinking ahead of itself? Are you overwhelmed by all the "things" you have to do? Do you get frustrated with slow moving traffic, finish sentences for other people or clean your mental laundry in the middle of a conversation with a co-worker? If so, you are employing what I call futurethink.

There are two kinds of thought about the future, productive and unproductive. Productive thought about the future adds to your quality of life and nurtures your loved ones, the community and the environment. Productive thought actually takes place in the present. Futurethink is unproductive thinking about the future and is harmful. Even if the outcome is positive, it always leaves us feeling stressed or unsettled. It creates anxiety, worry, stress, nervousness, dread and all number of phobias.

By definition, the future will never get here. The only thing you can know for certain is what is happening right now. Think of your mind as a rubber band. The more it dwells on the future, the more it feels stretched. Like that rubber band there is a breaking point. When the mind snaps you may suffer violent outbursts, migraine headaches, heart attacks, strokes or complete mental collapse. When you are innerthinking your mind is focused on the present, relaxing the rubber band and creating a calm, productive and vital mental environment.

Do you remember how it was to be a child? Let your mind float back to a time when you were very young. Find an early memory of you playing by yourself. (If you can't come up with a memory of your own childhood then simply observe a young child at play.) Remember how fluid and easy your play was Remember how totally absorbed you were while playing with a doll or tow truck, watching a ladybug crawl upside down on your finger or lying in the cool grass while the silent power of the of the earth slid you under the billowing clouds above?. You were totally aware and completely content. The key to being an adult with a child's heart is the same—learning to pay attention to what you are doing right NOW!

Let's try an exercise to demonstrate the value of innerthink. Think about something in your future that upsets you. It might be a relationship, money, your job or your family. Pick a particularly troubling scenario and pay attention to how strongly you feel it. Grade the intensity of this future worry from 1 to 10, with 10 being the worse-case scenario. Now we are ready to begin.

Experience Three
How to overcome anxiety

Hold your hand out and look at it. Observe it for what it is, a hand. Do not entertain judgments like, "My hands are too small" or don't add commentary like, "I remember when I broke my little finger." Just look at your hand as if for the first time, or as if it belongs to another person. Note the texture of the skin, the way the skin forms around the knuckles, which finger is second longest. Slowly make a fist and see which knuckles bend first. Feel the muscles and tendons working inside the hand when you do. Wave your hand through the air and feel the breeze between your fingers. Rub your hand on your arm and feel the sensation of skin and hair on your palm. Then observe what the arm feels as your hand passes over it. Explore an object (A pen, a glass, or whatever is handy) by feeling it with your hand. Pay attention to the vibrant world of sensations and feelings, especially the feelings this object gives you. Do this for 3–5 minutes.

When you pay attention to what is happening right here and now a wonderful transformation takes place. Think back to the experience you just had. During the entire exercise were you worried, upset, angry, sad, or anxious? Did you have thoughts about not paying the bills or about someone who has mistreated you? Immediately after you finished the exercise did you feel mentally awake, physically relaxed along with a general sense of well-being? When you are completely absorbed in what is, it cannot happen any other way.

In your mind, revisit the future event that you graded from 1 to 10 before doing exercise three. Grade it again. If you were absorbed in exploring your hand, like a child at play, you will find that you now have eliminated, or at least greatly reduced, your anxiety level!

It is impossible to worry about the future when you are paying attention to what you're doing now. This is not deception or denial. You are not running away from your troubles, quite the opposite. Dwelling on the future, while ignoring the present, is the ultimate form of denial. It is the unfailing formula for anxiety.

Something else profound has happened here that you may not even have noticed. You were the pure observer. You, the Self, was there observing at the same time your mind was thinking and your body and senses were interacting with your environment. You were a quiet witness to what was taking place. This is the key to living a life free of tension, worry and guilt. This is inner-think. Attention on "here and now" revitalizes the mind and revitalizes the body. Paying attention is the soothing salve that will cure the countless ills of human kind.

Whenever you feel anxious, worried, frustrated or stressed you are practicing futurethink. The antidote to futurethink is innerthink, bringing your mind back to the present. Pay attention and let your senses invigorate you. Step outside and look up. Observe how the clouds and birds are supported by the sky. Don't just look at the sky, look into it. Feel its depth and expansiveness. Notice how it makes you feel deeper and more expansive. Close your eyes and listen to every sound from every direction. Pay attention to everything, all day long. At the end of the day you will have more energy because innerthinking saves energy. You will be stunned at the strength and beauty and joy that blossom in your life just by being aware.

Boredom becomes impossible

Until now the exercises have brought your thinking to the present so that you could get to know your pure Self. They showed you that you are not the mind or the body, but a presence that is beyond things and thoughts.

By paying attention you have the best of both worlds. Your Self is the observer, the quiet witness, watching the tender beauty of life unfold. The Self is not involved in doing. It is just enjoying the ride. This I Am, your essential nature, is old and wise. It knows the doing will get done with no effort needed on Its part.

When you lose the Self and get caught up in the hustle and hassle of the phenomenal world you begin to suffer. Simply by observing, the harmful effects of mindless activity are neutralized. Not only does observing defuse stress and anxiety; it actually enhances our effectiveness at work, home and play.

When you are innerthinking you receive support from everything that is connected to the Self. Since your Self is infinite and unbounded it is connected to everything. When you are observing, you are paying attention to what is happening right now. You are not having thoughts about how late it is, did you remember to turn off the lights or should you have sushi or crab cakes for dinner. Your thoughts reflect what is going on right now. When you are inner-thinking you will see what is taking form at that very moment and watch as it becomes an integral and functioning part of the whole. It is beautiful, awe-inspiring and completely normal. Innerthinking makes the mundane new and boredom becomes impossible.

The future will take care of itself

Every moment is complete in itself. Everything that is needed to make the moment successful and to complete your life is in this moment. Every instant of your life is shimmering with effervescent pearls of wholeness. All you need do is watch for them. And then, all you need do is continue to watch as they blossom into the wondrous people and events that define your life.

When your mind is elsewhere, when you are not paying attention to what you are thinking and doing right now, you will miss the beauty that unfolds beneath your wings. When you try and manipulate the circumstances of your life you do so with your mind. And, as we have already seen, your mind is only a part of creation. It does not have the big picture. I have heard it said that a little bit of knowledge is a dangerous thing. In this case there is no question of it. When you pay attention to the present the future will take care of itself. Try it. You will be amazed.

MAIN POINTS FOR CHAPTER SIX

How To Fix The Future

- Futurethink is unproductive thinking about the future. It creates anxiety, worry, stress, nervousness, dread and all number of phobias.

- It is impossible to worry about the future when you are paying full attention to what you are doing now.

- Dwelling on the future while ignoring the present is the ultimate act of denial.

- The antidote for futurethink is innerthink, bringing your mind back to the present.

- When observing the present with complete attention, boredom becomes impossible.

- Every moment is complete in itself. Nothing more is needed for you to be complete but to observe the fullness of this moment.

- When you pay attention to the present the future will take care of itself.

CHAPTER 7

Your Problems Are
Not The Problem

*"Is not life more than food, and the body more than clothing? And who
of you by being worried can add a single hour to his life?"*

Matthew 6:25, 27

The homeless mind

A few weeks ago I was approached by a homeless man. Some time earlier I would
have turned away, or handed over just enough money to make me feel better. But
this time was different. I stopped to chat as with a friend. He asked me for money
to buy a hot dog at the 7-Eleven. I asked his name. Slight surprise registered on his
face and he told me his name was Thomas.

I asked Thomas questions I wanted to know about him and he was eager for
the conversation. He told me how he had lost his home and about his fears for the
future. He said his life was full of anxiety, and guilt and mistrust. I told him that I
have friends who are millionaires who have the same fears.

As he told me more about his life I listened intently. He talked about his past,
then the future and then more about his past. From his past he dredged up guilt,
remorse, sadness and grief. His future vision reflected anxiety, tension and dread.
These feelings from his past and future were alive in him as we spoke. His eyes
focused past me as his mind played the movie that was his life.

After some time, he stopped and looked at me for words of consolation. I smiled
and asked him, "Where are your problems right now?" He stood a moment in
silence. Then he replied, "I lost my home and I have no job, and I..." "Right now!"
I said. "What problem is causing you to suffer this very moment? When you stop
thinking about your past and future you are left with just this moment. How do
you feel right now?"

"O.K., I guess." He mumbled.

When I asked you "where are your problems right now?" you paused for a second and then started playing your "problem" tape again. You didn't pay attention to what was happening just then but rather restarted your future/past thinking again. During that brief silence, while you were pondering my question, you had no problems.

"We all have circumstances that challenge us. Not having a home or job are circumstances. Circumstances are not problems. They do not become problems until your mind attaches useless and damaging emotion to them. It is the homelessness of your mind that has created your pain. How much is being jobless helped by worry? How much is being homeless helped by lamenting the home you used to have? Circumstances are real. Problems are made in the mind.

"Let me ask you again Thomas, Where are your problems right now? What circumstance is so overwhelming that you can not enjoy this moment with me?"

He paused longer this time as his vision turned inward. Soon his face relaxed, a reflection of the shift in his thinking. Then, tears began to well up and he said, "I feel good right now. I know I still have problems, I mean circumstances, but right now I feel lighter and peaceful."

"Right now, we are sharing what it means to be human." I told him. "We are right here with each other, free for this very moment. By paying attention to what is happening now, our minds come to rest on this moment. And this moment is always more peaceful and productive than the fear-driven fabrications that our mind dreams up. The night sky is clear, the breeze is soft and the sounds of the city are soothing.

"What is the use of worry? To stop it, you only need to embrace this moment. When your mind runs from the past and races to the future it forgets the present. And, the present is the balm that heals the mind of problems." We spoke a little longer and then Thomas gave me a big hug, turned on his heels and disappeared into the night, completely forgetting about the hotdog.

Several evenings back our paths crossed again. We began to speak as old friends. He told me that he had secured two part-time jobs and started going to church again. I told him that he had changed my life as well. "It feels good," I told Thomas, "to rediscover my Self in your eyes."

Problems do not exist in nature

What are problems? I suppose they could be referred to as difficulties, setbacks, obstacles or generally some condition that in some way interferes with our intended goal. Problems do not exist in nature. It takes a human to create a problem.

We humans tend to see a problem as something outside of us. We feel that other people, things or circumstances are the cause of our discontent. Once we identify a problem we set out to eliminate it. All the while feeling that happiness is just the other side of the problem and if we vanquish it we will be happy. Beyond that, tucked somewhere back in the shadows of our mind, lives the hope that if we eliminate all our problems we will come to know eternal happiness.

Do you know anyone who does not have problems? Do you think we will ever run out of them? It appears that there is a basic flaw in our thinking. If some part of our mind tells us that we will be happy when we are problem-free, and we agree that it is unlikely that we will never run out of problems, then we must finally face the fact that we will never be ultimately happy.

You might point out that problems allow us to grow and evolve. What will we be evolving into? Obviously that would have to be unhappy problem solvers. Whenever we conquer one problem another one rises up in its place. The sense of peace and accomplishment fades quickly as we prepare for the next battle. Life becomes defined by a series of trials, setbacks, crises, predicaments and troubles with occasional flashes of peace and happiness. Is this all there is to life. Is this the way it was meant to be? I don't believe it is. I don't think that you do either.

The key to unraveling this mystery is in our perception. I am not implying that all you have to do is change your thinking. This has never worked to our complete satisfaction. You could try replacing negative thoughts with uplifting ones or you might tell yourself over and over that you really are at peace with the world. You may even try to understand the motivations or circumstances that created the trouble. Or you may just give in and write it off to karma. None of these approaches will have much of a lasting effect on your overall happiness. They are mental models built on the shifting sands of the mind.

The autothinking mind creates problems. So the problem is not the problem. The problem is the mind. The mind is the source of all disharmonies. Shakespeare said, "Nothing good or bad but thinking makes it so." The answer lies in fixing our thinking. But how do we do that? By thinking about it? If we try to fix the little problems by using the big problem, the mind, we simply create more and more problems. When we look to the world to solve strife and discord we are the victims of misdirection. No official proclamation for world peace has ever worked. No government can proclaim peace for its citizens. The citizens must do that for themselves. A peaceful world blossoms from individual peace, not the other way round.

Individual peace can become reality only when you step outside your individual mind. At that very instant problems cease. You stop making problems for you and for the rest of us. Innerthinking breaks the wheel of karma and it bears you beyond the influence of the stars. When you begin innerthinking you have stepped outside the negative influences that have created such frustration, friction and discord for you.

Appreciating nothing

Finding your Self is easy. We can do it whenever we want. If just being present eliminates all our problems, and it is so easy to do, then why do we continue to suffer on such a monumental scale? Indeed, why does anyone suffer at all?

It pretty much boils down to a matter of understanding. Understanding nurtures appreciation. And we have not been able to appreciate the subtle, and yet remarkably profound influence that innerthinking has on our world. Knowing how to innerthink is a diamond in the rough. Don't toss it casually aside. Do not overlook the power of being present to transform your life from fear and frustration to joy and love.

Although we don't like to admit it, instant gratification seems to be the banner around which we have rallied. Technology has offered us a phenomenal array of labor-saving devices, toys and amusements. TV, the opiate of the masses, is now useless without a remote control. The pace of living is approaching warp 10 and our ship is falling apart at the seams. We are screaming headlong into a future that has no meaning other than to separate us from our past.

Innerthinking on the other hand is quiet, pure and lacks identity. For that reason it is deceptively easy to undervalue the absolute transformation that takes place when we remember our Self. At least this is the case in the beginning. It is the opposite of what we have learned to value. Self is not something we can grab hold of with our hands or our minds. We cannot use it to overpower or control some objectionable part of our life. It doesn't work that way. It simply is what It is. And that is how It works.

A watched pot never boils

As you remember, our actions and perceptions are directly influenced by our thinking, our thinking by our feelings, and our feelings by how secure we are. If we are present, that is if we are paying attention to what is happening now, we are secure. If we forget I Am we are not present. When we are wrapped up in our thoughts and I Am is forgotten, we become insecure.

When we are present, we are aware of what we are thinking and doing. Where are we when we are not observing, when we are autothinking? Why, we get caught in psychological time. In other words, we get lost in our minds.

We know that our mind creates time. And, we know that this mind-made time is the cause of our problems. The next question should be, "Why would the mind do a thing like that?" To find the answer, we have to take a very close look at the most refined part of the mind. We have to watch what happens as the unbounded I Am first begins to take the form of mind.

I Am is pure and without form. But, it is the origin of all things in the cosmos including our mind. There is a point at which I Am starts to warm up and something quite amazing happens. Something comes out of nothing.

When a pot of cold water is placed on a hot stove it goes through several stages before it begins to boil vigorously. First you will see convection currents in the water. The water appears thicker and wave-like as it is warming up. Then you will see the formation of very small bubbles clinging to the bottom of the pot. In time the bubbles get bigger, break loose and rise toward the surface. Finally, there is a great deal of activity as the bubbles get much bigger and the surface violently roils.

Creation of the mind goes something like that. As I Am warms up, waves are formed. These waves give rise to the tiny bubbles of thought. The tiny bubbles break loose from the bottom of the mind, so to speak, and head toward the surface of the mind. When they burst on the surface of the mind that is where we become conscious of our thoughts.

When the first wave-like movement of I Am takes place deep within the mind, I Am now says, "I Am mind." This is so incredible. I Am is still formless but it has also taken form as mind. I Am is stillness and mind is movement. Mind is moving I Am. I Am is stillness and movement together. In our boiling pot analogy the I Am is the still cool water. As it heats up and boils we see convection waves and then bubbles in the water. But these forms are nothing more than different expressions of water. It is all water. All of creation, galaxies and atoms, flowers and skyscrapers, you and I are all I Am in motion.

It is most crucial at this point that you do not forget that you are also I Am. Let's pretend that our convection wave caused by warming water in the bottom of the pot is alive. Let's say that it can think, act and react. It is important for this wave to remember that it was formed when cooler still water heated up. If the wave forgets that it is really moving I Am it will see itself as separate from all other forms of water. It will lose its unbounded perception of water and see itself only as a limited expression of water in the form of a convection wave. Then it will see itself as just a bubble. It will take delight as it expands and rises toward the surface. Our bubble knows from watching other bubbles that eventually he will reach the surface and pop. Pop is bubble talk for die. Now, analogies have their limitations and I think that we are stretching this one a little thin. But you get the idea. A human who forgets that she is I Am and focuses on her singular individuality will live an isolated life with the other rising bubbles right up to the time she pops.

On the other hand, if a wave could observe that it was both moving and still, then no matter what form it became, wave, bubble or pop, it would still be ever-present water. It would be free to enjoy the cycles of change without fear of the end. After all, when the bubble pops it just becomes formless water again. The end is just another expression of the omnipresent water.

When you practice innerthinking you are aware of I Am, and you gain the support of all that I Am is. You are not isolated to your physical or mental form and will not suffer when the body grows old or the mind grows dim. Because I Am exists beyond time you align with timelessness. Remember it is the mind that creates the illusion of time. It follows that, when your form and mind slip away and merge back into the ocean of I Am you still exist as your Self, omnipresent I Am. Herein lies the secret to immortality. For most of us our minds are a continuous boiling of thoughts. From the moment we awaken to the time we fall asleep our minds actively search out new things to explore or continue to rehash useless scenarios from our past. Mental static is the order of the day, every day. This hyperactive mind so common today that it is considered normal, wastes vast amounts of energy and continually gets us into trouble. Have you continued to think about something or someone so much that it starts to drive you nuts? Have you ever found yourself saying, "I wish I could just turn my mind off?" These "boiling thoughts" are out of control because you are identified with your problem and have forgotten I Am. When you stop thinking and then maintain awareness as thinking starts up again you have come into alignment with your Self. You will feel a calm wash over you. You will feel more energetic and creative and ultimately your life will become in tune with your needs and desires. Innerthinking is a wonderful freeing of spirit and the ultimate gift that you can give to yourself.

MAIN POINTS FOR CHAPTER SEVEN

Your Problems Are Not The Problem

- Problems do not exist in nature. It takes a human to create a problem.

- It is the emotion that we attach to a situation that creates a problem.

- Conquering problems does not bring peace. It only brings more problems.

- Many people define their lives by the kinds of problems they have.

- The problem is not the problem. The problem is the mind.

- The Self cannot be used to correct problems. However, when we observe the Self we live free of the negative influence of problems.

- When silent I Am begins to move it becomes aware of that movement and says, "I Am mind."

- All things in creation, including you, are moving I Am.

CHAPTER 8
How To Overcome Happiness

"When there is observation and therefore no movement of
thought—merely observing the whole movement of fear—
there is the total ending of fear."

J. Krishnamurti

Ego and the end of fear

Let us return to the ocean of silence, I Am. Now picture the first subtle movement,
something like the movement of warming water. I Am has now taken form. This
is the creation of mind. If I Am is aware of Itself as the movement of mind, everything is fine. But, if I Am, the ever-present Self, forgets Itself and only maintains
awareness as the mind, the primal problem is conceived. When mind forgets its
source it perceives itself as being completely alone. The first spark of fear ignites.
This first spark, born of fear, we call ego. It is here that we shall start our investiga-
tion into the workings of suffering.

Fear is spawned in separation of Self. When the mind forgets its Self, ego
becomes the controlling entity of the mind. Mind expresses the characteristics
of thinking, feeling and the very abstract quality of security. Insecurity drives the
ego. Ego uses thinking and feeling to try to recapture security. What ego thinks
it wants is dominion over all the "...beasts of the fields, and the fowls of the air."
In short ego wants to be Self. It spends all its energy and resources defending
and conquering. Since "everything" is infinite and beyond its grasp, ego cannot
possibly satisfy its hunger by feeding it one thing after another. This is the primal
mistake of the ego and the cause of all forms of suffering. Alas, ego is destined to
suffer miserably even when it thinks it is succeeding.

Ego never rests. It never feels content for long. It never feels whole. Ego gathers
things to itself to fill the emptiness left by separation from Self. Searching amongst
things is futile. For peace is never found in things.

Ego lives in fear. It is afraid that if it merges with the I Am its own existence will be annihilated. Fear is both its foil and its fuel. Ego separates itself from its foes so that it can identify and vanquish them. The idea of ultimate domination breeds a false sense of control. It divides and conquers, then falls into its own trap. More conquests bring more separation. From the sense of greater separation emerges still greater fear. Ego is a drowning man grasping at straws while he assures his would-be rescuer that everything is under control.

This simple misunderstanding is the source of world-wide conflict. The intellect is the part of the thinking mind that makes decisions. Under the influence of ego the intellect chooses the path of separation. What ego has done is to become its own authority. It is saying, "Let my will be done." When Descartes said, "I think therefore I am" he was supporting this split between the mind and the Creator of mind, a very grave mistake. Mind controlled by ego is not complete. It does not see the big picture.

Even when ego is happy it is worried

Wholeness is beyond the ego's capacity. Awareness of Self opens us to wholeness, the complete picture, and the ego has broken off its communication with It. Ego becomes the bully in the schoolyard bluffing and making boisterous claims. Like all bullies, ego is afraid. Ego is alone.

When ego feels separate from Self every thought, feeling, word and action is devoted to reuniting with It. But it has a dilemma. It does not want to let go of its own perceived sovereignty. And so the ego struggles to complete the puzzle of wholeness by forcing fragments of its life together. It gets a good job, makes a family, reads self-help books and never discovers the thread that binds them all together. Even when ego is happy it is worried that the happiness will not last. That is because it doesn't last. Pursuit of happiness and pleasure are shallow rewards for the joy and peace it renounced to become separate. In its frantic search for completion ego turns into a catlike predator. With a body of rippling emotions it pounces on the world baring the saber like-fangs of logic and analysis. But in the world of Oneness the laws of Darwin fail. True power is found in surrender, and evolution means returning to the primal state of innocence.

Time plus thought equals fear

Like a lost child in a wicked wood, the ego sees monsters in every shadow. The Bhagavad-Gita, a five-thousand-year-old text that helps us understand the problems besetting humankind, explains that fear is "born of duality." Duality dawns when ego sees itself as separate from the single Self. After separation it is ego against the world. Ego's sole purpose is to find its friends and foil its foes. The entire life of ego is devoted to this battle. It is always at war. This war can only end when ego surrenders its fear and is reunited with Self.

The study of the machinery of fear is a fascinating exploration into the ego's battle against unity. Mix all the colors of the rainbow and you get black. Mix all the common emotions, even those considered "positive," and you get fear. Contained within fear are the seeds for jealousy, anger, lust, grief, sorrow, anxiety, greed and so on. Nurtured by the waters of psychological time these seeds of negativity germinate and sprout into vines that choke out the tender shoots of Self-awareness.

Another name for fear is psychological time. Fear is born when thought begins moving to the past or future. Krishnamurti, a philosopher and spiritual teacher, lends us his equation for fear. His formula realizes that time plus thought equals fear. This simply means that when thought moves, fear is generated.

Remember that time is created by the mind, or more accurately, by the ego-influenced mind. Time is the illusion that there is a flow from past to future. A single thought, like the single frame in a movie, is only now. When the thought is done it no longer exists. If you remember a thought you remember it now. Your mind is telling you that there is a past but it cannot produce it. It can only produce thoughts in the present. Can you think thoughts in the past? Of course you can't. By definition, the past is gone. Time makes fear and fear makes time. And ego grows stronger with every thought of future/past.

The elimination of time is the elimination of fear. The elimination of fear/time brings the demise of the ego. How do we end time/fear/ego? Innerthink! We simply switch the mind off autopilot. That will stops consciousness from wandering down the future/past corridors of the mind. If we choose to visit the past or future we make sure that we bring along our Self as the observer. The observer is our anchor to the present so we do not get swept away in the river of time. Perform with complete attention any of the exercises presented in this book and you will instantly vanquish fear.

Now, let's take a closer look at what fear is made of. To do that we will build on the mental model presented earlier.

Driving Miss Crazy

We are going to introduce fear into the mental model. You already know that means also introducing ego along with time. If ego remembers that it is also I Am then we are secure, we are innerthinking. When our security is unwavering we enjoy healthy feelings and clear creative thinking. Our actions and perceptions then become harmonious with the environment and life is joyful and creative.

Ego however has other ideas. It wants to be the boss. Ego takes all the credit while doing its best to forget about the real boss, I Am. In order to forget I Am, ego invents time. Time, the future and the past, keeps our awareness from entertaining what is happening now. Awareness of "right now" stops time. Bypassing ego, our consciousness recognizes I Am as the real brains in the outfit.

By now you may be thinking that all this theory is interesting but how can it possibly eliminate my fear? It can't. That is the kind of thinking we humans have supported for millennia and it hasn't worked yet. Theory and thinking are no substitute for direct perception of Self. Understanding is a product of the mind. But we can only start from where we are. Because you are thinking, that is where we start. But we must transition to an awareness that is beyond thought. Theory has its value in two ways. First, holding onto ideas and concepts can be exciting but eventually you will have to admit that they do not of themselves bring peace. Upon this realization one is more likely to look for peace beyond the mind where it resides. Second, it may keep some of you interested just long enough for the experience of peace to take root. Then you can set the knowledge aside and just enjoy being your Self.

Fear is a dark, multi-faceted jewel

Now, let us attend to the task at hand. By most accounts the word "fear" is nebulous and ill-defined. And that's usually O.K. with us because of the strong feelings associated with it. It is like a dark multi-faceted jewel. A range of negative feelings reflect back as we view it from different angles. Turn the stone a little and we reflect anger, a few more degrees and we feel the glint of guilt. All reflections are painful to some degree or other. To deaden the pain we apply the anesthetic of mindless living autothinking. That is the barren balm of delusion encouraging the proliferation of fear rather than its demise.

If at any given time we become quiet and pay attention, we will find some level of emotional discomfort inside of us. It may be quietly working way off in the back of our mind. We just get used to it being around like the groaning of the refrigerator motor. Or it may be right in our face from the moment we awaken to the time we fall into fitful sleep. Most of us swing back and forth between the extremes.

There are those of us who are not aware of any discomfort because we choose to ignore it. We keep very busily focused on the matters of our lives. We may be workaholics and proud of it. We may also deaden the relentless fear with alcohol, drugs, sex, food or other addictive activity.

Our shadow lives are thrown against the backdrop of fear but occasionally, or frequently, it erupts to the surface as anger, guilt, boredom, worry, etc. Our experiences of pleasure and happiness seem slow in coming and never stick around long enough for us to truly be at peace. Pleasure and happiness, as we shall see, are the ego's devious devices to make us think that we are making progress. The question is, progress to where? And when will we get there?

No matter who you are, where you are or what your life situation is, you can go beyond fleeting pleasure and happiness and live in complete peace and joy. The answer is not out there nor, is it in your mind. It is in your awareness right here, right now.

Feelings and eu-feelings

What is the difference between anger, pride, worry, sorrow and other feelings and the eu-feelings of peace, joy and bliss? Simply put, feelings have reasons for existing and eu-feelings do not. If you are angry you are angry for a reason. For instance you may be angry with your spouse for squeezing the toothpaste tube from the top. You may be sad because you lost someone. You may be worried because you can't pay the bills. There are conditions for all feelings whether we are aware of them or not.

Eu-feelings (short for euphoric) are unconditional feelings. They do not have or need a reason for being. They just are. For instance, peace exists wherever we are at all times. When you are innerthinking you will experience peace along with whatever else you are thinking or doing. You may even recognize that it has been there all along but you haven't been paying attention to it. Peace is your natural state of being when you are not caught in the emotional milieu of conditional feelings.

Conditional feelings are creations of the mind and caught in time. They serve the needs of the ego to divide and conquer. All conditional feelings have opposites, for instance happiness has sadness and love has isolation. And they are always associated with the past or the future. Eu-feelings have no opposites. They come from beyond the mind. They are expressions of our true nature. They are reflections of Self-awareness in the mind.

Other eu-feelings are silence or stillness, joy, bliss or unconditional love, ecstasy and the experience of the awe of oneness. While eu-feelings stand on their own they can produce conditional feelings in the mind. The experience of pure joy is waiting for you to discover it. It waits for you beyond the mind in the experience of I Am. When you experience pure joy it may arouse feelings of pleasure or happiness in the mind. The eu-feeling from beyond the mind is perceived as happiness in the mind. In this case the conditional feeling "happiness" still needed a reason for being. That reason was the eu-feeling joy. Conditional feelings like anger and lust produce other conditional feelings. But conditional feelings can never produce eu-feelings.

This is a very important point to ponder. We must discriminate between feelings generated in the mind to appease the ego's need for dissension and the eu-feelings that support infinite harmony and peace. If we do not, we will remain chained to the whirling wheel of emotional turbulence that has brought our world to the threshold of annihilation. Once understood it is easy enough to remedy. Experience first the universal harmony of peace, joy and love and let the healing unfold spontaneously from within.

Fear—The wolf

Fear is a feeling. Actually fear is the sum total of all conditional feelings that you have collected during your life. That is why it is very hard to identify that uneasy gnawing feeling that follows you around like a shadow. That fear may be a mixture of one part guilt, two parts frustration, and seven parts worry. To complicate things even more, that general fear melds with others, and those with still others until you have created the granddaddy of them all, which we just call fear. Given this simmering stew of feelings and our tendency to avoid uncomfortable emotions it is no wonder that we have become emotional morons. But we shall be morons no more. The cure is near at hand. It is nearer than your next breath. It is closer than your next thought.

When time appears in the mind it takes on the shroud of future and past. The fears that accompany time can also be divided into future and past. Eckhart Tolle in his book *The Power of Now* has categorized them for us. If your thoughts are dwelling on the future you may experience some form of worry, unease, anxiety, nervousness, tension, dread, stress or pride. You will find yourself asking, "What if...?" If on the other hand your thoughts wander to the past, your feelings will include guilt, regret, resentment, sadness, self-pity, bitterness, non-forgiveness or grief.

"Well," you say, "when I think about my daughter coming to visit I feel happy. That's a future thought." That is very true. But if you examine the thoughts that come along with that happy thought you will always find negative ones. For instance, you may be happy she is coming but you worry about her safe journey or if she is over the disagreement you had last time she visited. And you may wonder with some irritation if she is going to bring along that goofy guy she's been dating. The same is true with thoughts of the past. You may have a fond memory but thoughts of sadness, regret or some negative emotion will also be there. You may have trouble recognizing them. They may hover just beyond your conscious awareness, but they are there.

Happiness—The wolf in sheep's clothing

To make matters worse, the cunning ego has devised the cruelest trick of all. The positive feelings of happiness, pleasure, excitement, and yes, even love, create greater suffering than the negative ones. The ego is truly the master of illusion.

Happiness is not really happiness. We must understand this point completely. It is an illusion. Happiness is disguised suffering. It is a specter. It is a tantalizing mist that cannot be grasped by the hand.

How can this be? How can the very feelings that we dedicate our lives to accomplish actually cause us such great suffering? The answer is simple. Happiness and pleasure are conditional. They only appear in our lives if conditions are favorable. And who decides what conditions will bring us happiness? Why, our old nemesis the ego.

Still confused? Let's take a closer look at happiness. What makes you happy? Is it a new car, more money, a newfound love? Sure it is. If someone handed me a million dollars right now I would be elated. Happiness is that good feeling you get when something goes your way. Pleasure, delight, satisfaction are just different degrees of happiness. I will use the word happiness to include all positive feelings.

We cannot say that happiness is the opposite of fear because happiness is a part of fear. Without happiness fear would be only a cold, black lake ever lapping at the shores of your mind. It takes the high-minded winds of happiness to create the fury in fear.

It is natural for all life to avoid pain and move toward pleasure. This behavior is genetically encoded for the survival of all species. It came with humankind and has been operating before the first glimmerings of self-awareness. It is a survival instinct, to be sure. But in man it has evolved into a search for Self. For anything less than the realization that I Am causes only a deeper longing for union with Self. Union with Self eliminates pain. It heals the wounds of time and bathes the soul in infinite Bliss.

Union with wholeness is what we are seeking. That is not what ego is offering. Ego offers suffering in pieces. Happiness is a piece of suffering. Happiness is dependant on circumstances.

You cannot control happiness

I love the story of the child who decided to become a millionaire. "I will be the richest man in town," he promised. "I will be respected and envied and they will erect a statue of me in the center of town. I will be a great success and live happily-ever-after." And so he left the town and began working on his plan that very day. He kept his nose to the grindstone, his shoulder to the wheel and his eye on the goal. Finally, at the end of his life he had saved a million dollars. He was ecstatic that his life-long plans had been realized and that he would gain the recognition he deserved. When he finally lifted his nose from the grindstone and shoulder from the wheel and returned home, he found that oil had been discovered beneath the little town and all the townsfolk had become billionaires.

Most of us make silent pacts with ourselves. They can apply to anything like choosing a mate, buying a bagel, or learning to speak Spanish. But money is the easiest example for our purposes. The pact might go something like this."If I make $1000 dollars this week I will be happy. If I make $900 I will be less happy. If I make more than $1000 I will be very happy." How did you decide on $1000? What factors went into the final decision? What happens if you make $2000 and have it all taken away in taxes? You see? Your happiness depends of so many circumstances you cannot possibly control them all. So you can never control happiness, for the variables are infinite. Is this not your experience? Do you see anyone around you who is controlling happiness? It cannot be done.

Happiness cannot be controlled but that is not what causes suffering. It is the belief that happiness needs to be controlled in the first place that spawns heart-ache and sorrow. As soon as you believe that you are not happy you have already lost the game. If you believe that happiness has an opposite, i.e., suffering in some form, you now have two things. You are playing the ego's game of duality.

When you are presented with two things you have to decide which is better for your purpose. You have to judge one better than the other. You decide to pursue one and eliminate the other. Then you qualify your choice like we did with the $1000 example. It is a vicious cycle that endlessly repeats itself every second of every day of your life unless you are innerthinking.

The human innate desire for wholeness is distorted by the ego's need to preserve its own existence. Under the ego's influence the mind feels that primal drive toward unity and interprets it as a quest for happiness. Logically it thinks it must eliminate the bad and increase the good, when in reality all that is needed is to innerthink.

Ego thrives on diversity. It needs conflict to survive. The greater the conflict the more ego feels alive. So it spins the illusion of duality, of positive and negative feelings, friends, fortune and fame. As long as we live the illusion of diversity we will suffer as ego grows stronger. The instant we remember I Am, all suffering ends. It is our choice. We truly can choose to suffer or be free of it. Despite our experience to the contrary, it is the illusion that happiness will somehow pluck us from the murky whirlpool of emotions that keeps us swirling ever downward. Believe me, it does not matter which hemisphere you are in or if the whirlpool rotates clockwise or counter-clockwise. In every case the result is the same, pain and suffering.

Even when we appear to be happy there is a wee voice in the back of our minds saying, "This won't last. Get used to the idea that it will soon evaporate. Unhappiness is coming. You will soon feel alone again." Is this our reason for being planted on this planet? To experience a long life of struggle, to momentarily reach some tenuous pinnacle of pleasure then slide down the other side into more struggle? I don't think so. Neither do you.

Great! You've lost all hope

I have often been told that when hope dies all is lost. To which I reply, "You cannot live free of suffering until you lose all hope." Hope is another great hoax cooked up by ego. Hope is a creation of time. I think you will agree if you take a minute to examine it with me.

When we start a sentence with, "I hope..." what are we really saying? We are affirming that the future will be better. Whatever we desire and don't have presently will be provided us in the future. What do we know about the future? It doesn't exist. It will never exist. Hope, like happiness, is a flickering star beyond the grasp of all except fear-inspired imagination. It is unobtainable in any real sense of the word. Hope and happiness do not exist except in the entangled tendrils of psychological time.

A person who tells us that he has no hope usually means that he has given up trying to reach a desired goal. In the search for Self, this is actually a very good thing. At the moment that he stops creating an effort to obtain what he wants, he begins to get what he needs. He opens himself to help from sources other than his limited self or ego.

The instant he surrenders, all activity stops. His mind is still. It becomes open to whatever may take form out of silence. He is at an impasse but he hasn't given up. He is just waiting for the universe to make the next move. He has yielded to Universal Intelligence.

Arjuna and the Song of Life

The Bhagavad-Ghita is often called the "Song of Life." It is a story of good over-throwing evil. But ultimately it is a story of seeking and finding Self. Its teachings are as applicable today as they were at its writing 5, 000 years ago. As the story begins the two great armies, representing the forces of light and dark, are gathered on the battle-field of life. At the head of the army of light Arjuna, the main character, is poised to do battle against the mounting storm of negative forces. His job as an archer is simple. He must slay the ruling negative forces so that the righteous regain influence over the earth. But Arjuna has a serious conflict. In order to do his job on the battlefield he must kill family members, teachers and friends. They have come under the influence of powerful negative forces and have taken up arms against the forces of good. This scenario is not unknown to us even today. Many good people, whether out of desperation, fear or ignorance, have thrown in with tyrants throughout history. The most vivid example in my mind, is the Nazi war machine where millions of well-meaning people were driven by their inner suffering and a fervently irrational hope for a better world.

So what is Arjuna to do? If he fights for good he will kill his family. If he does not fight, negativity will sweep over the earth. Arjuna is a man of great intelligence, balanced by a deeply compassionate heart. Sitting there in his chariot between the gathering storm clouds of good and evil, he simply cannot decide. Completely lost, Arjuna drops his bow and surrenders to the moment. He knows his mind alone is not sufficient to resolve this dilemma. He also knows that Universal Intel-ligence, the greater Self, can. As soon as Arjuna surrenders he creates a gap in his thinking. In this stillness he is not trying to work out his problems. Nor is he creating harmful and distracting emotions like anger or self-pity. His surrender creates a space for universal order to filter in and open his awareness to the solu-tion. And this is exactly what happens. Arjuna's Self takes form as Lord Krishna and compassionately lifts his vision beyond the importance of problems.

This remarkable scene takes place in the first chapter. The rest of the Bhagavad-Gita is devoted to resolving the problems that humans create. Basically it warns us that our problems are not the problem. Our limited minds are the problem and we must stop thinking long enough for the light of Self to illuminate our actions. Then when we start up our thinking again it will be with the support of universal order, beyond problems.

A side trip to visit God

I want to take this opportunity to diverge from the path a bit and try and clear up any questions you may have about how I comprehend God. It is not important that you know God the way I do. That is absurd. You can only see God through your own eyes and that is as it should be. There is value in the saying "God speaks to each of us differently hoping that we will tell each other." I share my perceptions with you for two reasons. First, like a flower or a rock or a deep blue sky, it is another expression of God that you may find of personal value. Take it for what it is, a simple sharing from one human to another. Second and more functionally, understanding how I see God will help remove any confusion as to how I use words and phrases like Self, I Am, perfect order, inner peace, pure intelligence, presence or absolute silence. For our purposes here these words are synonyms and you can use them interchangeably. Do not get stuck on the words. No word can describe or give you an experience of God. My job is to approach God from many different directions hoping you will be inspired to fill in the gaps with your experience. On one level we can say that God is like the hub of a bicycle tire. All the spokes lead to the hub. I am presenting as many spokes to God as time and convention allow. I may suggest a path but the journey is yours alone.

Another way to look at God is that It is the hub, the spokes, the tire, the air in the tire and the inherent function of the tire. This second view is closer to my experience but my writing reflects both approaches simultaneously. You won't be completely at home with either. That you will find on your own.

At one time in my life, God appeared to me in form, much as Krishna did to Arjuna. Since that time the form of God has dissolved into unbounded space, beyond time. There is a saying that all things, great and small, crumble into dust before the oncoming feet of the Lord. For me, "all things" included the idea and form of the Lord as well. In fact, I see all form as made of waves of energy and that energy unfolds from formless presence. Things are not solid to me. They are vibrating emptiness. At times I wonder why the table just doesn't vibrate into non-existence or the sidewalk crumble beneath my feet. It is somehow strange and yet completely natural and very comforting.

When silence is particularly intense, the distance between objects appears to diminish. I have many times felt that I could reach up and pluck the moon from the black sky and examine it like a pale, clear gem. Every thing in the universe knows every other thing, not by communication between them but by a non-moving Knowingness. Boundaries that make an automobile different from an anteater take on a secondary role as the presence that permeates them and surrounds them also unifies them.

Physiologically at these times I feel like space moving through space. When I walk it is as if the air passes through me, not around me. My joints are liquid and loose and I seem to glide effortlessly from here to there. Every cell in my body is like a flower drinking in the radiance of silence. I feel nurtured and completely safe.

You may have noticed that this is the first time that I have used the word "God." This single word brings with it many preconceived ideas and conflicting emotions. It tends to create confusion, something we need no more of. Do not attach to the word whether it be God, or silence or perfect order. Words are ghosts and should not be mistaken for the things they represent. Likewise, things are ghosts and should be seen as such. Do not mistake the gift for the Giver. Or more accurately, do not mistake the gift as the totality of the Giver. For me to attempt to define God is the ultimate exercise in futility. Ask me who or what God is and I will tell you that I do not know. My definition of God is simply this, "Unknowable." To me this is the highest knowledge, to not-know God. Thomas Aquinas said, "All the efforts of the human mind cannot exhaust the essence of a single fly." Anthony De Mello, a Jesuit priest with a penchant for analogies (a man after my own heart), quoted C. S. Lewis as saying, "It is like asking how many minutes are in the color yellow," De Mello elaborates the point by exposing the ridiculousness of discussing the qualities of God. He says that almost everyone takes the question seriously. "One person suggests there are twenty-five carrots in the color yellow" says De Mello "the other person says that there are seventeen potatoes, and they're suddenly fighting." If the greatest knowledge is to know that you don't know, then the greatest ignorance must be to think that you do know. The illusion you know God will keep you chained to limited perceptions and ideas and your mind will exert great energy in the effort to squeeze God into your mental mold.

My experience of God leaves me with the feeling that I know nothing and everything makes sense. That is the best I can do. The best I can hope for in my writing is to use descriptive, yet emotionally neutral words and analogies that allow you to transcend the rigors of thought, and ultimately experience your own God in your own way. That said, let's get on with the business of being hopeless.

Back to being hopeless

In your prayers you may have asked for the Divine to work through you, to make you a tool in the hands of Divine Will. How do you think this is done? Do you think that Divine Will is going to overpower your limited, self-indulgent will and force you to behave? It doesn't work that way. Why would a universe of infinite order stoop to our level by using force? How could you ever learn to go with the flow of life if you were forced to do so?

When we hope for something to be different than it is, we are creating force against what is, against universal order. We are saying that what exists right now is not good enough and needs to be changed. In essence, we are telling Universal Intelligence that It goofed up and that we want It to fix Itself in our image. That is a little on the self-centered side, don't you think? That might be O.K. if we could back it up with successful actions but our track record in this regard is pretty dismal.

When we are left without a direction we frantically try to find one. It seems that we crave direction, even if it is the wrong one. When we lose direction we panic and dive headfirst back into the fray, into the emotional pool of frustration, guilt and self-pity. We feel that we must always be doing something. We feel that doing nothing must be avoided at all costs and yet it is from Nothing that everything comes. (More on this in chapter Fourteen—How to Not-Know.)

When I say that I have no hope I mean that I have given up trying to do it myself. But what is it that I have given up? I prefer to replace the phrase "give up" with the word "surrender." Surrender means we are not looking to the future for things to get better. It means we are aware of Self and are waiting to see what options will issue forth from that state of infinite possibilities.

Arjuna did not give up. He simply stopped muddying his mental waters and waited for Divine guidance to shine through his un-muddied mind. He surrendered. Arjuna retreated to a state of alertness but without thinking or performing action. Does that sound familiar? The exercises in this book have first taken you to this state of surrender of thought and action. In that state of silent witnessing, your thought is guided by nothing less than the full organizing power of universal order. Hope is not an issue.

Every instant has contained within it the solution for that moment. When we are looking hopefully to the future we miss the answer that is offered in the present. We love it when things work out the way we plan them. That is, we want life to line up the way we think it should. If it doesn't, then we judge it as "wrong." We are looking for a solution our way. This narrow view excludes answers offered that fall outside our spheres of knowledge and experience.

When you are autothinking, your mind becomes a prisoner of its own creation of time, separated from the timeless whole. It becomes a piece of the whole. When you are innerthinking your mind reconnects to the whole. It becomes Wholeness. As soon as you surrender your limited view of life, you automatically fall in phase with universal order. At that very instant you will feel stress, tension and dread draining away to be replaced by eu-feelings like stillness, peace and joy. The order of creation flows in your favor. Now you are free from the agony of your labors. Every second of your life is fresh with wonder. Your struggle ends when you surrender to what is and simply watch as It unfolds your life before your eyes.

MAIN POINTS FOR CHAPTER EIGHT

How To Overcome Happiness

- Ego is the first spark of fear.

- Ego tries to regain security by manipulating and controlling things.

- All emotions, even happiness, come from fear.

- Another name for fear is psychological time. Time makes fear and fear makes time.

- The elimination of time is the elimination of fear.

- Feelings are conditional. Eu-feelings are unconditional, generated by Self awareness.

- The greater the conflict the more ego feels alive. The illusion of happiness creates a dramatic contrast which vividly enlivens ego.

- Having no hope means surrendering to what is here, now.

- Every instant has contained within it the solution for that moment.

CHAPTER 9
Memory Is Not Intelligent

*"The significant problems we have cannot be solved at the same
level of thinking with which we created them."*
Albert Einstein

When you think a thought where does it go?

When you think a thought, where does it go when you are finished with it? Interesting question, isn't it? That question might spur a few more like, "Where did it come from?" or "Are there different kinds of thought?" and "Does thought influence my thinking or my feeling, and if so, how?" If your right brain is dominating right now you may also be asking the question, "Who cares?" If you are, stick with us for a while longer. I think you will find our upcoming discussion completely captivating.

Let's look at the first question a little more closely. Where do thoughts go? Thoughts are mental energy. Once a thought has been thought, does that energy dissipate and merge back from whence it came? If it did, then there would be no record of it ever existing. As it turns out that is not the case. A record of thoughts does exist. It can be found in the mind. We call it memory.

Before we go any further we need to be clear on a couple of terms to avoid making a very simple notion harder to understand than it is. Thinking is going on right now. What you are thinking is taking place in the present. Thoughts on the other hand happened in the past. Thoughts are past thinking and they are stored in the memory. So *thinking* is done in the present and *thoughts* were produced in the past.

Scientists tell us that every thought we have ever had is stored in our memories. When we forget something it has not been erased from the memory. We just cannot bring it into our conscious mind at this time. Just because we have forgotten something does not mean that it does not have an effect on us.

Unconscious thought causes a whole lot of trouble in our lives. In fact, unconscious thinking is truly the cause of all our problems.

We know about unconscious thought. That is old stuff stuck way back in the memory somewhere. But how can we have unconscious thinking? Aren't we aware of what we are thinking right now? Ninety-nine per cent of the time NO, we are not. This is called autothink. And herein lies the problem.

Memory is me

In Chapter One we explored the difference between "I"and "me.""I"we said is universal and without boundaries. "Me" is made of the specifics that we commonly use to define ourselves. "Me" is who we are, what we do, what we believe, who we love, etc. "Me" is memory. If we only know "me" we merely know limitations that expose only fleeting glimpses of who we really are. If our minds are frequent visitors to the past we are dwelling in memory. The thing that keeps "me" from knowing "I" is memory. "Me" is past. "Me" does not exist now.

Memory superimposes thoughts over thinking. "I" is covered up by "me." "I" is pushed out by our past. And we already know that the past does not exist. "Well," you say, "if the past doesn't exist then how can it affect the present?" That is a great question. The answer to which can free you from the chains that bind you to the past, and even the future.

When thinking about the future or the past, when are you thinking it? That's right, you are thinking about them right now. It is impossible to think in the future or the past. But it is entirely possible to think about the future and past. Thinking about something is done right here in the present. So you see you do not have a past. You only have a memory of it. And you are having that memory now. It is an illusion. It is a dream that past "me" is more important that the present "I." If you buy into the illusion, you are living a dream. If you don't, you are awake.

Isn't memory necessary for our survival? Yes, memory is a very powerful tool and absolutely necessary for our continued well-being. And now that we have fingered the memory as the bad guy I have to say that it really isn't the memory's fault at all. If you fall asleep at the wheel of your car and it goes off the road, is it the fault of your car? Someone has fallen asleep and let memory run amuck. Your memory, like your car, is a tool. It needs to be guided and cared for.

If memory has taken over then who has it taken over from? Who is not paying attention? Why, "I", of course. "I" is present awareness. When "I" begins to believe that It has a past it becomes "me." It buys into that illusion and begins to build an elaborate matrix that supports the mirage. When "I" falls asleep our old nemesis ego sneaks in and takes over. While "I" is not paying attention ego uses memory to convince us that the future and past really exist and that they have substance and meaning necessary for our peace of mind. Are you beginning to see how clever and distorted our needy egos are? The past tells us that we are not as happy as we could be now. But if we do the right things or love the right people we will be happy in the future. Many of you may be falling back asleep right now. You may have found yourself saying, "That's right, I must prepare for my future happiness." See how easily we slip into autothink? Earlier you experienced "no thought" and then learned to observe your thinking. You may have been thinking about things in the future or past but you were aware of your thinking as it was happening. "I" was observing "me." You were innerthinking.

Autothinking is the opposite. Autothinking is when you forget you are thinking. Your mind then goes chugging off in all directions, wasting vital energy on the illusion that happiness is just beyond the next thought. That's a bit like a man dying of thirst and crawling through the desert toward a mirage. He can see the cool, life-giving waters right in front of him but he never quite reaches them.

Here is a good example to show the difference between innerthink and autothink. Have you ever read a paragraph in a book and when you got to the end you couldn't remember what you had read? Your mind was future-pasting and not aware of what you were doing. Even if you were analyzing or judging what you were reading, you were autothinking. When you are simply reading and paying attention to what you are reading, you are innerthinking. That's it. That is the simple difference. And that simple difference will save our collective bacon.

Memory is not intelligent

Memory is not intelligent. Memory is marvelous for automatic things like walking, driving a car or remembering your name. For instance, when I ask you your name you answer quickly without thinking. If I ask you what you had for breakfast yesterday it takes you a little time to answer. You have to "search" your memory for the answer. Searching the memory is an amazing process and not at all what it seems.

We used to think that memory was like taking a picture of any given moment, an exact snapshot of what is. Researchers have discovered that the memory is not at all static. As it turns out memory is a very dynamic process. It cannot be relied on as an accurate depiction of reality. Memory, it turns out, changes to fit our needs and desires. In one piece of memory research investigators showed a driving safety film to the subjects who were asked to pay attention to detail. At the end of the short film subjects filled out a questionnaire. One of the questions was, "Did the motorist stop before or after the stop sign?" Some observers said before and the rest said after the stop sign. In actuality, there was no stop sign at all. In order to answer the question each person's memory filled in the missing details. Memory molded its response to fit circumstances. Our memory is more like a digital image on our computer screen than the fixed images found on film. With the right software we can get rid of red-eye, lighten or darken the picture and add or remove people until the retouched picture barely resembles the original.

When I ask you what you had for breakfast yesterday there is a little gap in your thinking while you "remember." The gap is not unlike the gap you experienced when you stopped your thinking in exercise one. If I ask you a more difficult question like, "What is the meaning of Life?"the gap will be longer,the stillness deeper. We generally don't focus on the space between thoughts because we are looking for the answer to appear. In fact, so intent are we on the answer that we may even consider the space between the posing of the question and appearance of the answer to be somewhat of a nuisance, or even unproductive.

Did you ever have the experience of knowing that you know the answer but it just will not rise into your consciousness? You might say that it is right on the "tip of my tongue." The harder you try to remember the further it recedes into the inaccessible reaches of your mind. Then when you stop trying, the answer comes. Why? Why when you left it alone, did the answer pop into your consciousness with such ease and clarity? The reason is because your memory is not static, not chiseled in stone.

Your memory is a liquid and pliable tool. It takes the form that is most advantageous for the user. The user is either your ego or your Self. Your ego uses the mind to collect and control. It fights against silence like a child fights against sleep. It jumps from thought to thought looking for the magic combination that will make it king. Ego is chaotic and fragmented.

When your memory floats in the silence of Self, however, it gains the support of unbounded wholeness, peace and order. The Self actually reorganizes memory so that the answer can surface. The memory is not intelligent. It is the silent Self that gives us the answer through the vehicle of memory.

When you are involved in an argument with someone your mind fires off thoughts like bullets spraying in every direction. Ego has taken over completely. Silence has been silenced. You are running off memory and memory is not intelligent. You are autothinking and may find yourself saying ridiculous, hurtful or even childish things that you would never say otherwise. When the argument is over and you are walking away, you start to settle down a bit. As relative quietness starts to return you might find yourself saying, "I should have said...to him. That would have really nailed him." As more time passes and you continue to quiet down, more silence infuses into your mind and you are less driven by your emotional past. At this point you may feel some compassion for the other party and start to find solutions for the original problem. Now your memory is switching from ego driven to Self-supporting. A mind that is quiet and reflective is incapable of harm.

Memory is always outdated

As soon as a memory is made it is outdated. The information that goes into making a memory, the thinking and feeling, the sensory input and spur to action changes from moment to moment. You might say that some things never change but that is not true. Everything is always changing. The fact that we may not perceive the change does not mean that change has not taken place. There is a saying that you cannot step into the same river twice. Even if you step out of the river and immediately back in, the water that flowed by your feet the first time is already downstream. The same is true with making memories. A millisecond after a memory is stored the circumstances, feelings and people and objects related to the event have already changed. You cannot step into the same event twice.

Autothink is the acceptance of memory as present. It is saying that all the things that define "me" have been updated to this very moment. But that is obviously an illusion. If memory is outdated and you derive your sense of who you are from your memory then you are outdated. That's right. You are not current. You can never be current when you relinquish control to your memory.

This is a heck of a pickle that we have gotten ourselves into. Ego-driven memory is driving us insane. So what can we do? Can we lay our memory on a couch and ask it questions about its childhood? Of course not, analysis in this case is a complete waste of time. If our mind is broken then we cannot use our mind to fix it. That truly is insane. And that is exactly how we are approaching all our problems, not just the mental ones. If the memory-identified mind has made the problems, then fixing the mind will fix the problems, not the other way round.

If autothink is the problem then innerthink is the solution. Innerthink does not accept the stuff of memory as present. When we are paying attention we are not running on memory. We are not outdated. We are current. And when we are current we realize that the memory is there as an advisor and not the ultimate authority. Memory simply makes suggestions that we match against the present conditions. If memory's suggestions fit we use them. It they don't then we revise them.

I once met a woman who was a hairdresser from Colombia. She had been in the U.S. for several months and spoke almost no English. She smoked cigarettes and drank strong Colombian coffee from morning till night. She worked long hours, ate little and poorly and had a host of physical complaints related to her lifestyle. When I went to get my hair cut we would nod and smile and I would show off my command of the Spanish language by saying "Hi" and "Thank you very much." I once tried to ask her how she was feeling. What I actually said sounded more like, "Your bed has feelings." I knew by her vacant expression that I had better stick to pointing, nodding and a lot of smiling.

She was a pleasant woman and I was somehow drawn to know more about her. I remember my ego subtly nagging me that there was no sense in getting to know her because (and now ego seizes the moment and the memory to support its argument) I shouldn't be around smokers or people who abuse themselves by overworking and poor diet. She knows no English and I know no Spanish. Furthermore, she comes from a totally unfamiliar cultural and vocational background. Even if we could communicate, what would we talk about? "After all, Frank," the ego urged, "You need to have 'deep' conversations to satisfy the intellectual appetite. Anyway, aren't most of the people from Colombia involved in trafficking drugs?"

Boy, what a crock! I couldn't believe my thoughts. It was hard to accept that they were coming from me. Or more accurately, they were coming from the ego-manipulated memory of "me." Well, I just continued to observe these mental shenanigans as the ego unfolded them. I didn't fall into its trap and identify with the way I had seen things in my past. I did not interfere as the ego spun its web, drawing filament from the stuff of my memory. I just watched the process unfold without interfering in any way.

The three profound advantages of innerthink

Innerthinking, observing without interfering, in this way gave me three very profound advantages. First, by not participating I did not lend my current mental energy to the momentum of my past prejudices. These old stored mental tapes have energy of their own. In the past, I freely gave in to ego believing that it would be used to make me happy. Deceitful ego took my fresh mental energy and used it to strengthen the illusion of hope and happiness. By observing the ego in progress the downward flow of vital energy is halted.

Second, by stopping the flow of vital energy to the ego, the ego becomes feeble and loses its influence over our minds. Sometimes the stored emotional energy in our memories is very strong indeed. When emotions are in control you feel out of control. You may have decided to go on a diet and not eat any more sugar. Then when it's time for a snack you find your mind telling you that it would be quite all right to have a piece of that donut calling out to you from the coffee table. Then you hear, "I really shouldn't have any sugar." And in reply, "I've been so good and one piece won't hurt all that much." Two minutes later you have started your third donut despite the bitter taste of guilt.

This mental tug of war of "should I or shouldn't I" is between past and future. In the past you gained too much weight so in the future you will not eat sugar and therefore lose that weight. You think that if the part of your brain that wants to lose weight is stronger than the part that wants to eat sugar, you will lose weight and live happily ever after. Sorry, Charlie. They are two sides of the same coin and even if you win, you lose.

This drama between "good" and "evil" is staged for your convenience by your old nemesis ego. It is all smoke and mirrors. It is designed to divert your attention from the real source of joy and love, attention on the present. Even if you possess great will power and lose all your fat and become a walking billboard for health and beauty, you will continue to be tossed around by the polarities of your mind. You will have to wrestle with the mental mechanisms of pride and vanity. And now that you are physically beautiful you must fight to stay beautiful, which we all know is a losing battle.

By entering into the ego's fray you add momentum to its cause. Essentially, ego is a nonentity. It is like a shadow. It exists only because we feed it energy. If we stop feeding it ego will wither and die. Not feeding it means not dancing the future/past fandango. The ego does not get fed when we simply observe without being drawn into the drama.

Have you ever had a one-sided argument? It can't be done. If someone wants to have an argument with you and you don't participate then there is no argument. Your opponents will try and push every hot button you have. At first they will be confused. When they realize that you are there as an observer and not a participant they may double their efforts to draw you into combat. Their ego greatly fears your non-participation because it constitutes a loss of control. If your opponent were to start observing, then his ego would cease to exist too. Eventually, with no participation from your side the challenger will eventually exhaust himself and leave you alone. But if you just once fire back a salvo of insults, complain or try and explain your position, they come back on you with renewed vigor. It is the same with the ego. The more you feed it the more powerful it becomes. When you witness without interaction the ego will weaken and eventually die. The ghost of the ego will remain forever a pale reminder of the danger of the dance.

The third profound advantage of observing is absolutely ingenious. When you innerthink, the stored energy in the memory that was used to deepen the illusion of personal progress is converted to strengthen pure presence. The more you observe the easier it becomes to observe. It's money in the bank. Once converted this spiritual energy is never lost! Even if you fall back asleep and dream the ego's dream you will never lose what you have gained. Like a trip of many days, when you fall asleep at night you wake up where you went to sleep, not back at your starting point. When you again awaken to the Self it will be at the same level of pure awareness. Waking up becomes increasingly easier until you reach momentum. Then it becomes effortless.

Colombia on my mind

Several weeks later I had occasion to share a table with the Colombian hairdresser in the smoking section of a crowded restaurant. I listened patiently as my mind reeled off the reasons I should not be in the smoking section with a smoker who didn't speak English, and with whom I had only my hair in common. I continued to observe my thinking as I sat down and smiled through the long and awkward silence. "This is the menu." "Yes"..."Good food." "Si"..."Crowded restaurant.""Yes"... And so it went, morsels of our lives sandwiched between thick slices of silence until the meal had ended. All the while, I watched as outdated objections jostled for dominance in my mind. Never interfering, I watched as they bubbled up and burst on the surface of my consciousness. Then I saw it. When the bubble burst it became silence! What a remarkable observation. Memory was past energy, trapped and stagnant. When put into motion by the manipulative ego it could motivate me to act in a similar manner on those damaging thoughts. I could have reacted to those malicious thoughts streaming out of my memory and continued to strengthen this cataclysmic cycle of negativity to be relived again and again. Or I could clearly observe them coming and going. As I remained awake and inno-cently watched the process unfold a wonderful transition took place. The negative thought energy stored in the memory when not reacted to, converted to a subtle healing energy I recognized as my own inner essence, my all-accepting Self.

This is what burning the seeds of Karma in the fires of attention means. For seekers following the dictates of Eastern philosophy, knowing this can liberate you. Living in pure presence frees one from the illusion of Karma and of birth and death. You may have heard that the enlightened have broken the "wheel of Karma." You may have read that the wise are no longer subservient to the influence of the stars. This means that the forces identified by astrology no longer control your destiny. Observation of what is will free you. You may have tried to think only "good" thoughts and perform only "good" deeds hoping to neutralize your bad Karma with good. You could have created an atmosphere of non-violence and not even slapped a mosquito sneaking a free lunch. The badge of Ahimsa is not reflected in how many itchy welts you have accrued. Without pure presence all these efforts are empty. Aren't these practices just variations of the future-past fandango? Didn't Christ say that we can not get into heaven by good deeds alone?

Tossing the tip on the table, I felt a deep sense of calm as if everything was just as it should be. If I had listened to the echoes of my memory, I would have been sniffing my clothes for smoke and mentally highlighting the awkward moments that dominated an otherwise innocent adventure. Instead I was at peace. During the months that followed I learned more about the Colombian I had broken bread with. We eventually became friends and parts of my life have been greatly enriched because I chose to observe, rather than react to the mania of my memory.

MAIN POINTS FOR CHAPTER NINE

Memory Is Not Intelligent

- Memory is "me."

- You do not have a past. You only have a memory of it. Memory is thinking about the past while you are in the present.

- Autothinking allows past thoughts to dictate your present actions.

- Memory is not intelligent.

- Memory changes to fit your needs and desires.

- Memory is always outdated.

- When you are aware of the present memory simply becomes a tool that offers suggestions that may or may not be useful at this present moment.

- The three advantages of innerthinking (1) decreases negative energy

- (2) weaken ego's influence (3) strengthens awareness of Self.

- Observing the Self will weaken and eventually eliminate ego.

CHAPTER 10
Fixing A Broken Mind

"The human race has been doing it for ages. It notices that something is wrong, but it doesn't find the right cause."

David Bohm

Insanity runs in my family

Insanity runs in my family. Take it easy, Mom; I am speaking about the Family of Man, the human race. In the old days when we only had clubs and spears we could not inflict widespread damage on ourselves or the earth. If our race does expire it probably won't be with a nuclear "bang" as we thought in the 50's and 60's, but rather with a "whimper." If humanity does not first yield to a natural catastrophe like an asteroid collision or spewing volcanoes, it will surely succumb to the autothink virus. The antidote is innerthink. It is cheap, in fact free, and available to anyone who has a mind. We start by slipping beyond the menace of the mind to experience inner peace. There is no reason for a single human not to be experiencing inner peace and prosperity. A quiet shift in perspective is all that is needed. Let's now take a closer look at how our minds unwittingly betray our most vital need.

David Bohm is one of my favorite philosophers and has had a profound impact on my life. He was a quantum mechanical theorist of the highest magnitude. Einstein called him his "intellectual son" because his process of thinking was closely aligned with Einstein's. Niels Bohr and Einstein made invaluable contributions to the New Physics in the first half of the 20th century. Because of poor communication between the two men they did not actively support nor enhance each other's work. Bohm saw this as a grievous waste of talent and a great loss for humankind. Bohm spent much of his life examining the mind and how it related to itself and the "external" world. He felt that if he could find out how the minds of Einstein and Bohr had broken down then the world could be spared a loss of that kind in the future. The result of his research was, like the man, pure genius. Bohm discovered that the mind creates a problem by the way it thinks. Then the mind blames the problem for causing the trouble. And then the mind tries to fix the problem, which is only a symptom of the misdirected mind. He says that we think that the problems are out there. The mind thinks that crooked politicians, poor schools, the dying environment and unemployment are problems that need to be fixed. "But," says Bohm, "people's attitudes create the problems and attitudes come from the *way* we think.

We think that someone is the way we feel about him. We don't realize that how we feel is our constructed image—not real—or more real than another person's feelings. The solution is to see how we are *now* thinking—to watch our mind as it is working."

Bohm had discovered innerthink. His approach to the subject is original and insightful. Throughout the rest of this chapter I will draw from David Bohm's ideas to add emphasis and clarity to my own.

Autothinking is thinking without awareness of your Self. When you think about something, your mind convinces itself that it intimately knows the object it is thinking about. So there is just your mind and the object. There is no observer of this process of thinking that is taking place. Let's say that you are looking at a rock and your thoughts are about that rock. Your thoughts about the rock are not the rock itself, are they? Your thoughts about the rock are only thoughts which are in your mind. The rock is not your mind. Autothinking is thinking that says your thoughts represent the rock exactly as it is. It says that the rock in your mind is exactly like the real rock. You think that how you see the rock is how it really is. This is a kind of ownership that is encouraged by ego. But in reality, a rock is a rock. A rock is not your thought about the rock. Do not mistake a thought for a thing. This can only get you into trouble.

The cycle of desire

When you look at a rock or a person an impression of that object is carried into the mind through the senses. When an impression enters the mind it goes into the memory. There it stimulates that part of the memory that pertains to that impression. When you are walking across the street and hear a car horn blaring behind you, it creates impressions in the memory that have to do with similar stored experiences of horns and cars and so on. Your memory then creates the proper response to the impression. In all likelihood you will jump out of the way, shake your fist and yell a few choice expletives and then go home and change your pants.

Between the times an impression stimulates the memory and you perform the appropriate action, the memory creates a desire. In the example above the jumping to safety is a reflex where no desire was needed for action. The desire came afterwards when you wanted to throttle the driver of the car.

Let's look at another example. If you see a box of candy on the table and smell chocolate, you will probably have the desire to eat one. When you see and smell the chocolate those impressions travel through the senses of sight and smell to your memory. Your memory then creates a desire and that desire then spurs you to action.

Senses → Impression → Memory → Desire Action.

The action created from desire will create more impressions for the memory to create more desires and actions and so on. As you can see it is an automatic process. When this process goes on unobserved it will create many problems for the owner of that mind. In this example you may consume half a box of chocolates before the desire to stop is initiated. Performing action purely from memory is insanity. Awareness of this process as it unfolds is its opposite. I am sure this is what Socrates was telling us when he said, "The unexamined life is not worth living."

How to create: A silent word from our sponsor

Last night I stopped writing and went to bed. While I was asleep I was aware of my dreams, as sometimes happens. As I watched my surreal dream unfold it reminded me of a kind of bizarre television soap opera. (Actually, I think that using the word "bizarre" to describe soap opera is redundant.) Anyway, as I lay watching my television dreams a voice broke in like a commercial. Quiet and clear as a bell it said, "Tell them why they have desires."

There were no more instructions but I knew when I sat down to write again this morning the explanation would be there. All I would have to do is write down what flowed from the depths of my Self. To do that I just turn my attention to the silence between thoughts while remembering the question, "Why do we have desires?" I did just that and silence began to bubble. The bubbles began bursting on the surface of my consciousness as the explanation was typed out on my monitor. The following words are boiling consciousness. Pour them in your cup and sip slowly. Mixed with spices from your own mind, it will produce a medicinal brew that will soothe the pangs of desire. This is a recipe for peace. Try it using your own ingredients.

While we are a little off course, I would like to walk just a little further along this path and talk with you about my perception and how it may impact your life.

It will be different for you but the basics will be the same.

As I write I am many times surprised and delighted at what appears on my monitor screen. I am at the same time author and reader. This is the joy that all artists and performers feel while expressing their craft. Writing is so much fun that I can't wait to sit down and begin. Please understand, I don't go into a trance or call on other forces to do my bidding. On the contrary, I am deeply and simply aware of silence, and that is all. I have learned that silence will produce the most wondrous gems if you simply watch and wait. I love Eckhart Tolle's description of this powerfully innocent state of attention mentioned earlier. He says we should be like a cat watching a mouse hole. That simile perfectly captures this subtle state of curiosity.

When most of us experience pure silence we say, "So what?" and turn our minds back to worldly distractions. The first time you stopped your thinking in exercise one and were left alone with No-Thought, you may have been looking for some "thing" and missed No-Thing. As you continued to do this exercise, the moments of silence became longer and deeper. Your body began to relax and your mind let go. It was followed by a greater appreciation for this simplest state of being. Looking into silence is like looking into a deep clear pond. At first glance you see only the water on the surface. But as your eyes focus beyond the surface, you begin to see a beguiling world just beyond your reach. And so it is with inner silence.

I don't look for anything. I just wait for what comes out of silence. I think this is the deepest meaning of the saying, "All comes to he who waits", or "...to he who is Silent." What takes form is for me. I am writing for me and sharing it with you. When you read these words you pick up the essence of pure silence as it is mirrored in me. You will resonate with some of what I say, but not all. You need not create effort to draw benefits from this book, quite the opposite. Simply accept what you resonate with and let the rest go. The second time you read this book you will be amazed at how much more inner peace you will have. That is because what you originally resonated with has now blossomed like the opening petals of a flower. And that beauty inspires other sleeping "buds" in you to awaken.

When a musician writes and then performs a piece of music, she imprints her personal expression of inner silence on that piece. When the audience hears her work they resonate with her individual reflection of creation. The mood of the music strikes a resonant chord within us and we become the music. Pure silence created the musician, the music and the audience. The music is the song silence sings, awakening in us our very Selves.

Instead of listening to music you are reading this book. The mechanism is the same. You may have noticed that as you read through these pages you feel lighter, more peaceful or even spiritually inspired. Like each note of music, each word plucks the strings of silence within you. As you continue to read, your ability to be present and experience silence in your daily life grows exponentially. This silent order is inherent in the words because "me" sat down and observed while silence did the writing.

I do not attribute what I am sharing to a higher "Being." In my world there are no higher beings. We are all equal. We are all the higher Being. It has to be so. If God is everywhere all the time, then He/She/It must be Us. I think we are just here to remind each other of that fact. My writing this book is my way of reminding me. Your reading it is your way of reminding you. And in that way, this book is our music.

Breaking the addiction of desire

We were examining how an impression from our senses or other thoughts and feelings, creates activity in the memory which in turn produces a desire. The desire then creates feelings and thoughts which spur us on to action. Feelings, thoughts and actions open the mind to receive new impressions and the cycle begins all over again. Thoughts and actions are intended to alleviate desires. But this is not what happens.

The autothinking mind is the ego's workshop. In such a mind, impressions enter the memory and come under the influence of ego. Like a malicious magician, ego masterfully manipulates the impression's impact on memory and creates the great illusion, a new desire. These desires like "I need more money" and "I want someone to love me" serve to strengthen "me" and weaken "I." Each desire is a stone cemented into the foundation of failure to find harmony.

Let me just take a second here to distinguish between a desire and a preference. A preference is something you prefer. Between the colors blue and green you may prefer blue. A desire is ego-driven emotion. It is something you feel you want or need to make some part of you more complete. Desires spring out of memory and bring with them a host of supporting thoughts and emotions. If you have ever bought something you didn't need or did not have the money to buy, you know the difference between preference and desire. Preference is simple and pure. Desire is clouded and convoluted. A preference you can take or leave. A desire creates yearning and craving.

Impressions do not have to come from sensory input or from the results of action. They can be created by desire alone. If a desire is unfulfilled it will create impressions for future fulfillment. If a desire is fulfilled it creates impressions that spawn bigger and stronger desires. *It doesn't matter if you can satisfy a desire or not, autothinking continues to create new desires.*

We are caught in a cycle that cannot be broken by tampering with any of the parts. Trying to control our desires or impressions or how we react to them in the memory is futile. The unobserved mind is controlled by ego. Ego is sick but it is not stupid. Ego makes you identify with "me" and it appears that you have a separate identity. But if you think you are your past experiences, then you and ego are one. I have seen the enemy and it is "me." It is brilliant. It is insane.

It is not desire that we have to control. Desire is only a symptom of auto-think. Desire is created when we are not satisfied with what we have. Feeling unease, in any of its infinite manifestations, spurs the mind to seek solace elsewhere. Your mind may return to the past when things were better. Your mind might remember how glorious life was when you first fell in love or how much money you made before you were "downsized." Your mind may look to the future when you are sure to find a more attentive, lasting love or a better job with more money.

What do they say? "Money can't buy love." Money can't buy unconditional Love. Unconditional Love is a eu-feeling beyond the reach of money or manipulation. But conditional love relationships frequently revolve around money. The most common cause of strife in a relationship is money. (More on this in Chapter Thirteen—The Perfect Relationship.)

Why do we have the feeling that life is not complete? What propels the mind into the future or encourages it to slide helplessly into the past? At its conception, ego separates from Self and immediately loses the support of the creative compassion of that oneness. It feels the loss deeply and tries to complete itself by gathering things, like cars and houses and ideas and people. Ego collects more and more hoping to get the Most, which is exactly what it lost when it separated from Self in the first place.

Desire springs from the cloven heart of ego. Searching for wholeness, ego bends the mind this way and that. Moving this way, ego exerts energy to gather more things and increase control. Moving that way, it consumes great sums of energy trying to protect itself from the illusory monsters that it created.

Ego needs to be complete. But ego has a problem. The only way it can be whole is through its own annihilation. It doesn't want to give up its throne of power but at the same time it is driven to bow before the Self. It is no wonder that the single most common word used to describe our times is "stress." The multitudes of individual egos bumping into each other, jostling for a position on the top of the heap has created a frantic friction that has brought us to the point of spontaneous combustion. You can see ego's dilemma. It has a desire that cannot be quenched. When you identify with ego it also becomes your dilemma.

When we identify with ego we feel an unclear dissatisfaction from being separated from our inner source. It can be a general feeling of unease, restlessness, boredom, or anxiety. We persistently try to remove this discordant feeling by doing things. It is like a low-grade noise that we try and drown out by making a louder noise like overworking, drugs, sex, and the like. Even "good" activities create stress when unobserved.

When you are present you unhook from ego. At this moment of quiet attention, while you are "watching the mouse hole" you reach the goal of all desires. Every desire was created out of ego's need to be complete. When you observe you are complete. Thoughts and feelings and actions become secondary in importance. Life choices become preferences. Because you have awareness of the whole you do not desire the parts. The parts are at your disposal and become a source of creativity and joy. There is no need to strive for fleeting happiness. Your desires are fulfilled the moment they arise.

Fixing a broken mind

If a part breaks in the engine of your car you replace the broken part with a new one. The broken part represents a breakdown in order. The new part is more orderly than the older broken part, as it relates to the closed system you call your engine. When the new part replaces the old, the whole system becomes more orderly and your engine purrs like a kitten. When you went down to the local car parts store and came back with the new part, you were actually going outside the broken, closed system in order to fix it. You could not fix your engine by taking out a broken part and putting it right back in. Neither would you find success by replacing it with a new broken part. Your engine wouldn't work and your neighbors would stop dropping by. You wouldn't treat your car engine like this. You would think that anyone who did would be rowing with only one oar in the water. Yet that is exactly what you are doing with the mind when you "fix" a problem.

All right, I guess we cannot go down to the local mind parts store to replace a broken mind part. Or can we? Can we step outside the mind and come back with a replacement for ego? In a manner of speaking we can. Innerthinking is stepping outside the mind while it is still running. It is like turning on the broken car engine to see where the problem is. And here the analogy begins to break down a little. We can step outside the mind and observe it working. But there is nowhere to go to get a new part. There is nothing you can *do* to fix the broken mind. The fact is a broken mind is fixed by "not-doing." Simply observing a broken mind will fix it! That is the point. It is the not doing that fixes everything. Or more accurately, it is in the observing that you realize that it is already fixed. Observing ego while it works its devilish tricks means that it can no longer get away with them. Ego must work in the secret in the shadows of your mind. Ego is shadow. Observing ego ruins all its fun. Paying attention to the workings of your mind is like turning up the rheostat on a light bulb. As the light gets brighter and brighter the shadows grow dim and eventually disappear. There is nothing to fix. Only increase vigilant awareness and the shadows will be seen for what they really are, the absence of Light.

Your mind is the light bulb. The electricity that creates light in the bulb is awareness. Answers do not come from your mind. They come from awareness. Awareness is the pure expression of creativity and order. If you think that your answers come from your mind then ego has put another one over on you. The mind changes awareness into thought like the bulb changes electricity into light. Light comes from the electricity passing through the bulb. Thoughts come from awareness passing through the mind. The answers to the problems facing human-kind come from innerthinking which is simply observing pure awareness as it passes through in the mind.

The menu is not the meal

When we autothink a rock we think that we know what it is. We label it "rock" and put it in the memory filed under "rocks." When we label something, we feel that we own it. That gives us a sense of power over the object. That reminds me of the native cultures that believe that taking a photograph of them captures their soul and imprisons it on the film. The older we get the more things we have labeled. Pretty soon the mind skips over life like a flat stone over water. Because it thinks it already knows the thing that it has labeled, the mind loses interest. It says, "I already know that thing. There is no need to look at it again." The phrase I hear so often that best represents this position is "Been there, done that." This is autothink, believing we have captured the soul of the object because we have taken a memory picture of it.

When something is labeled and stored in the memory it is immediately outdated and subject to deceptions cooked up in the memory. When you live by labels you miss the feast that is the now. It is much like being served a great meal in a restaurant. While a hot meal sits right in front of you, you are busy comparing it to the menu. "This doesn't look as good as #7"you proclaim,"But is has to be better than #14. Next time I'm going to try #43. That looks positively to die for." Mean-while, you have lost all interest in the real meal in front of you. It has become cold and tasteless. A cold meal cannot compete with mental menu fantasies.

When we innerthink, the labels remain but they do not influence what we are experiencing at that moment. In other words, the past label does not diminish the joy of observing that object as it is now. Watch a young child who has not learned to label. That mind is interested in everything. Innerthinking puts memory on standby while it observes the mind and the object as if for the very first time.

Almost every thought has a feeling attached to it and vice versa. By looking for the emotion that goes with the thought you will begin to see the motivation behind the logic. I am not pointing this out to you so that you can better control your life, but for you to observe the genius of your Self as it is reflected in the mind. It is truly remarkable.

Anger as a thing

Have you ever noticed that when you think about something that made you angry you get angry all over again? The event has ended, sometimes years before, and you still get angry when you think about it. How does that happen? This is also true with other feelings like guilt, jealousy, fear and revenge. How did you ever get into this fix? How shall you ever get out?

The problem is, we are thinking *about* our feelings. When we think about something we objectify that thing. Thinking about anger separates it from us and makes us think that we can fix it the way we would a car engine. We feel that all we have to do is change our behavior or remove the source of anger or think peaceful thoughts to neutralize the angry ones. In this case we are just trading one broken part for another. None of this will ultimately help. We may succeed in controlling or suppressing our anger or grief or dread for a while but this approach does not get to the source of these life damaging-emotions.

Bohm suggests that instead of thinking about anger we must *think* anger. Thinking about anger only revisits the emotions that are already present. In essence, thinking about a thing uses the labels that are stored in the memory. We are convinced that we are gaining new and valuable information about this person, thing or event. In reality what seems new is just a remix of what is already stored in our minds.

Thinking anger, on the other hand allows us to relive the incident so we can watch the machinery at work. As we watch we will naturally be drawn into it. We will experience the same feelings that we did originally and our bodies will respond to the anger in the same way. All negative emotions agitate the mind and age the body. Usually when a hurtful event is experienced like anger or fear or grief, we tend to re-live it over and over in our minds. This is life force for ego. Even if we don't want to think about it, it can take hold of us. We are helpless to make it stop. The most common way of dealing with unwanted emotions is to try and cover them up with drugs, oversleeping, mindless video games or TV or by "keeping busy." In this way, we are trying to run away from our minds. We want to excise that part of the mind that is causing the pain. We are trying to separate "me" from "me." That will never work. Separation from the mind is the right idea but that is not the way to do it. Now you tell me, how can we separate from the mind's domination over us? Of course, that is done by innerthinking, by stepping outside the mind by becoming an observer.

When anger first happens it is very fast. It is on us and before we know it we instantly begin acting out the anger. Somewhere in the middle of that episode, or shortly thereafter we realize that we are angry. Thinking anger lets us watch the event a second time, only this time in slow motion. When a fan is spinning at high speed its blades look solid. When we turn the fan off and continue to observe the blades we soon see that the solid blur was made of individual blades. Thinking anger is innerthinking as the machinery of anger is allowed to unfold more slowly than when it first occurred.

When you observe the anger machine do it without interfering or judging. Simply watch as it automatically unfolds. Do not have the intention that you want to get rid of anger. If you try to "fix" that specific event then you will have nothing to observe. A specific event of anger springs from other more general and deeply hidden emotions. Eliminating the single event will not remove the cause of anger. It only changes the way you feel about that one experience. The desire to analyze and surgically remove anger is ego's influence and will keep you chasing symptoms until your last breath is drawn.

Instead, you may feel the need to understand why anger is inside you. If you do, you will also be playing into ego's hands and be drawn back into the illusion through the intellectual side of the mind. So if you can't fix a feeling like anger or learn how it works, what can you do? Observe. That is simply all that is needed. When you innocently watch anger something magical takes place.

The spinning blades of anger slow down until they finally stop! Regular observing of the memory of anger or fear or guilt in this way will soon lead to the ability to observe the event as it is happening. Anger is automatically defused as it becomes a memory. While you will still have a memory of the event it will not carry with it the crippling emotions that bleed off your constructive life's energy. It's like watching the fog on your bathroom mirror disappear as you watch. Soon, without effort, all that is left is a clear reflection of your Self.

MAIN POINTS FOR CHAPTER TEN

Fixing A Broken Mind

- The mind creates a problem by the way it thinks. Then the mind blames the problem for causing the trouble. Then the mind tries to fix the problem it created, ignoring the fundamental cause of the problem, the mind itself.

- Impressions in the memory create desires which spur us into action. That action creates more impressions in memory, creating more desires, and so on.

- Ego creates desire out of its feeling of incompleteness.

- Desires strengthen "me" and weaken our appreciation of "I."

- Desires ultimately create more and stronger desires.

- As long as we feel incomplete, it does not matter whether a desire is satisfied or not, desires will continue to be created.

- When you are aware of the whole you do not desire the parts.

- Labels limit our appreciation of the object as it is right now.

- Observing a feeling without analyzing or judging, allows it to remain in memory without attaching debilitating emotions to it.

CHAPTER 11

Overcoming Psychological Pain

"I am finding the habit of life evermore joyful."
Johan Peter Muller

The Gate Technique

For me, God is formless; free of boundaries and yet interpenetrating all form. But this was not always so. There was a time when I associated with God on a very personal and practical level. It was then that I watched the majesty of the angelic realms unfold and sat in small groups absorbing the teachings of ascended masters. There were infinite levels of life both above and below my physical existence, and I learned from all those I came to know. These worlds were as real as the corporeal one I was born into. You might be quick to renounce them as an escape into a fantastic fantasy, as I did at first. You could, if it weren't for the remarkable tools and techniques that were passed on to me from those abundant realms. They remain with me today, more like memories of places I have visited on this earth. They are there but they do not draw me to them. I prefer the profoundly simple beauty of this world. It is complete as it is.

In the late 80's when God still had form, I asked to be given a technique that would quickly and easily bring peace to mind. The answer was the Gate Technique. I had been hosting regular meetings for a group of dedicated spiritual aspirants in my chiropractic office for some years. I remember that evening with particular clarity. It had been a bitterly cold, gray January day and I was surprised that anyone had braved the brutal Michigan weather that night. Nonetheless we had a full house. I had contacted the group earlier that week and let them know that we would investigate something new in the way of inner exploration but I was not specific. I was not specific because I had no idea what would materialize that evening, if anything. Settled in their seats the group looked at me expectantly. I sat there blinking back at them. God did not speak to me. In fact, He had been uncharacteristically quiet. Not knowing what else to do, I asked the group to close their eyes. We sat with our eyes closed for what seemed a very long time but in actuality was only about 10 minutes. I closely inspected the stillness for some sign of divine activity. The harder I looked, the further I drove the silence from me. Finally I gave up. I remember thinking that it would be a pretty short meeting this evening, at least the cookies and tea were nourishing. Then a form within the formless attracted my attention. Out of that silence my God appeared suddenly. In a flash of intuition I realized that I had been waiting for "my" technique to manifest so that "me" could stick another feather in "my" cap. As soon as I was sufficiently humbled, God made His entrance. On that bed of humility the teaching begin.

As soon as His splendid form was fully manifest, quite unexpectedly He dissolved back into Silence. I thought He was leaving me. And in a sense He was. He was becoming It, a process that would take seven more years to finalize. Then, out of that silence came the Gate Technique. As the group sat quietly I guided them in this procedure for removing mental suffering.

Experience Four
The Gate Technique

Sit in a comfortable chair where you will not be disturbed for 10 to 15 minutes. Close your eyes and let your mind wonder for 10 to 20 seconds. Now pay attention to your feelings. You may have some relative feelings like anxiety, frustration or are just feeling a little antsy. It doesn't matter what you are feeling just observe what is there for another 10 to 20 seconds. Now look for one of the eu-feelings. Examples of eu-feelings you might see are: silence, stillness, calmness, peace, joy, bliss or ecstasy. You may also see or hear other words like; light, love, compassion, space, infinity, pure energy, existence or grace. They will be there and one of them will stand out more than the others. If no particular eu-feeling surfaces, then gently pick one and easily pay close attention to it. Don't interfere, just watch.

As you watch your eu-feeling it may change in some way. It may get bigger or louder or fade away. It could change into another eu-feeling or disappear altogether. Or, your mind may shift to other thoughts or you may start listening to sounds coming from around you. You may forget that you are doing the Gate Technique for a while. If this happens, when you realize you were autothinking, you have already started paying attention again. Just continue to watch your eu-feeling without interfering. Or you can gently look for another eu-feeling and begin the process over again. It doesn't matter what happens as long as you purely observe what is unfolding before you. The thing is to just watch what happens no matter what is going on. Continue the Gate Technique for 10 to 15 minutes. When finished do not open your eyes quickly or jump up and start doing things right away. Keep your eyes closed. Take another minute or two to stretch and come back to the outside world slowly. Then slide easily back into your active life.

Physically you will be relaxed, possibly more relaxed that you have been in a long time. Psychologically you will be at peace. And what did you do to get this way? Nothing! Just observe. The Gate Technique teaches us to rely on nothing other than observation. What happens is quite magical. A deep healing begins without a glimmer of effort. Actually, effort of any kind is counterproductive. What the Gate Technique effectively does is bathe your psyche in the healing waters of Self. Self knows best. We are actually aligning with the wisdom of I Am. When done regularly, you will experience greater energy, physically and psychologically, more relaxation, less illness, more resistance to mental and emotional stress and improved relationships. All this is accomplished by simply paying attention. Very quickly you will notice that you are observing more and more outside of the Gate Technique, as you go about your everyday life. The Gate Technique is prefect by itself or can be added to the beginning of other practices to enhance their effectiveness. Done daily it will quickly establish the habit of observing in activity.

Melting moods

Up to this point we have spilled a good deal of ink on the subject of psychological pain. The mind is responsible for its own pain. Pain comes from nowhere else and can only be cured by slipping beyond the mind into joy, the mother of mind. Joy and peace, bliss and ecstasy are different reflections in the mind of the expressionless Self. These eu-feelings, as you remember are always present whether we are conscious of them or not. They are not dependant on our moods which change as our thoughts and conditional feelings change. It is quite simple. Conditional feelings unsupported by eu-feelings are the cause of the human condition known as problems. The problematic mind is confused, angry, fearful, suspicious and destructive.

It is time for you to stopped suffering. The solution is simple and easily within your grasp but it does require a little effort. It is merely a matter of priorities. Do you want to live a life of joy beyond imagination or do you want to continue to share your suffering with the rest of us? Only you can make this choice. You make the choice not once, but every second of every day of your life. Look at it this way. Most of us spend more time choosing our wardrobe for the day than we do toward ending our suffering. Begin from where you are. What you gain spiritually can never be taken away from you and your growth will be exponential. I guarantee it.

Excuse me a moment while I step down off of my soapbox. There...now let's get on with the matter at hand, relieving psychological pain. Think of a hose with a nozzle on it. The nozzle controls the way the water exits the hose. Turn the nozzle one way and a fine spray is emitted. Turn it the opposite way and the water stream becomes very focused and strong. The water represents your stream of consciousness as it is utilized by your mind. On spray setting the mist falls where the winds blow. Set it on "whoosh" and the jet stream cleans the debris from your sidewalk and driveway. Most of the time our minds are set on mist. Our thoughts are blown about by the winds of an unfocused mind. Momentarily we will learn to narrow our consciousness in an exact way that will wash away emotional debris. Mind you, I am not advocating concentration, analysis, free association or any other structured mental technique or therapy. The trick is to observe without control. In this way we surrender to the infinite organizing intelligence of Self. Psychological discord is created by "me" ignoring the wisdom of "I." Enlisting a technique that is "me" oriented will only make more problems. We are going to set up the mechanism and then let Self do all the work. That is the way it should have been done in the first place before we packed our psychological bags with so much pain. It will be like diving into a cool clear pool. All we have to do is lean over far enough on the diving board and let gravity do its work.

How to mood melt

In this exercise you will turn that talent of non-interference toward removing specific negative emotions that are lodged in the memory. These emotions continue to be a destructive influence diminishing the quality of your life.

Experience Five
How to overcome negative emotions
Sit in a comfortable position where you will not be disturbed for at least 15 minutes. Close your eyes and watch the flow of your thoughts. Now, let your mind entertain a minor to moderately negative incident. It can be from your past or an anxiety you may have about your future. Make the event very clear in your mind. Freely experience the situation, people and/or places that define the event. Identify your emotions one by one. Don't hold back. Allow them to grow stronger until they are as strong as they will get. Now grade the strength of the event that you are experiencing from 1 to 10. Ten would be the strongest you could feel.

Continue observing your emotions. One emotion will be stronger than the others. Examine this emotion closely. You may be able to feel it somewhere in your body or around your body. Find where the emotion is in your body. Observe it more closely. What color is it? What shape? What texture? Is there a sound or taste associated with it?

Now that you have located the emotion get out your mental magnifying glass and take a real close look at it. It is best to pay very close attention to how this feeling manifests, observing its qualities as described above. Keep observing ever more closely in this way and soon something about your impression of the emotion will change. For instance the color or location or shape might change. Or the emotion will weaken or strengthen or change into a different emotion altogether. You may have to watch it for several minutes before something changes, but change it will. When it does change, examine it even more closely. Look to see if the shape or size or color or texture has also changed.

Continue to closely observe the changes one after another. In time, sometimes quickly and sometimes not so quickly, a eu-feeling will spontaneously surface. Observe the eu-feeling as you did the negative feelings by identifying its shape, texture, location in body, etc. Soon you will experience a general feeling of lightness and inner peace. Practice Mood Melting for a minimum of 10 minutes (you can do Mood Melting as long as you feel comfortable up to an hour). If your mind wanders don't worry, it will. Just find the feeling where you left it and begin the observing process as before.

When you are ready to end the mood melting session, be sure to allow about 5 minutes just sitting, or lying with your eyes closed. This will give any un-dissolved emotions a chance to dissipate. When you have finished, revisit the original event just like you did at the beginning of this exercise. Again grade it from 1–10. You will experience a significant reduction in the level of emotional discomfort.

There is much more to Mood Melting than meets the eye. Sure, you feel great and you scored much lower on the 1–10 emotional index. But is this anything more than a warm-fuzzies generator? The answer is a resounding "YES."

When you observe in this way there will be a decided decrease in the intensity of the emotions that make up the event. Many of you will find that after just a few minutes the original negative emotions don't even register a 1 on the emotional scale. There will always be a decrease in the intensity of the event when you watch without trying to fix it or run away from it. (Running away is a form of fixing.) This is truly amazing! Merely removing yourself from the boiling stew lets you enjoy the smells and flavors that waft from the leftover memory. You are no longer one of the ingredients. You become the consumer, not the consumed. And now you are able to appreciate without suffering whatever meal life chooses to serve you. O.K., enough food analogies; I guess I'm just a little hungry. Excuse me while I grab a quick snack.

O.K., I'm back. Mood Melting erases old emotional tapes. You can bring up the same event tomorrow or next week or next year and it will remain on the lower end of the emotional scale. Not only that, but Mood Melting reached deep into the memory rooting out and neutralizing emotions that were linked to, but not consciously associated with the original event. Remember your memory is always changing. A specific event like the one you just used in exercise five is influenced by more general emotions like anger, jealousy and grief. There can be many different events associated with one general emotional memory. In turn, those general emotions are born of the single, primordial emotion fear. If you continued the Mood Melting exercise to its completion and found a eu-feeling firmly replacing the negative emotions then you effectively dissolved the general emotions. You also eliminated the fear that was reflected in the original event and any other events associated with that area of the memory. This is a very good thing. It means that you will no longer be bullied by hidden memories. The memories will remain but they will be devoid of their emotional charge. It is much like burning a rope. If you throw a thick piece of rope in the fire and watch till it is completely burned what remains is only the ash. The ash looks much like the original rope but it can no longer bind you. If you try to pick up the rope ash it will crumble in your hand. Your observed memories retain their form but lose the power to bind you. You may even find a smile forming when you visit a memory that once caused you much suffering. It has served its purpose. It made you aware.

Of all the exercises, Mood Melting requires the most diligence to enjoy the fruits of your non-labor. Please remember, this is an exercise in observation and therefore should be effortless. The key to Mood Melting is not to look for any particular results but to accept whatever results you receive. Any effort to control will only yield more suffering.

It is best to start with minor life disturbances. As you get the hang of this powerful technique you can move on to more troublesome events and neutralize them. In the beginning you may want to ask a friend to be a facilitator. He or she can ask you the questions like: What are you feeling? (Make sure you identify a feeling and not a generic condition. They are smoke screens that lead away from feelings. Look into the condition to find the feeling. Examples of generic conditions are: unhappy, tired, confused, numb, undecided, irritated, etc.) Is it in the body or outside of it? Where? What shape and color and texture is it? Does it make a sound? Does it have a smell? If you could touch it, what would it feel like? The facilitators ask only these questions, none others. It is vital that they do not introduce analysis, judgment, imagery or any other mind oriented technique.

Allowing someone to help you in this way will continually remind you to keep observing. In the beginning we may get washed away by thoughts and emotions and spend a good deal of time autothinking. Facilitators can abbreviate the Mood Melting process. They do not need to know anything about what is troubling you. You can keep all that privately tucked away inside yourself. I have helped scores of people eliminate disabling emotions and never knew what was specifically troubling them. The particulars are unimportant. A healthy emotional life begins with awareness of Self. That is all we have to know. The facilitator only need ask those simple questions about color, location, etc., that will help you turn your mental nozzle on "whoosh."

Sometimes, when you first approach a memory or a future event you will have the impulse to turn away. Remember the ego needs the dark. Consciousness awareness is light. When you begin to observe negativity you may find yourself saying "It is better to let sleeping dogs lie" and turn the nozzle back on spray mode. This is actually the result of ego's dark magic. When you first approach the event the problem may seem insurmountable. You may feel that there is no use in stirring things up because you can never work through such an uncomfortable and convoluted problem. This would be true if you were "working" through your problems. That is better left to the professionals like psychologists and psychiatrists. But you are not enlisting analysis or other mind modalities. You are stepping beyond the mind and simply watching what takes place. Ego hopes that you will be scared off by a hellish bogeyman from your past. You may initially feel a great surge of fear especially, if ego feels particularly vulnerable. Fear is the basal emotion, the emotion from which all others are born. When you hit too close to home ego will unleash a bolt of fear that can shake your very core. If you try and fix it, you are fighting fear with fear. You are trying to remove fear because you are afraid of it. Obviously that can't work.

When we observe we are not trying to fix anything. We are watching to see what happens. You see, we are mistakenly living by laws that are first established by filtering through the biased perception of ego. By witnessing the process without interfering we remove ego's distorted influence. Observing is the beginning of problem-free living. There is no fixing needed. We have already arrived. All that has been built on deception will become clear. We need do nothing. There is an ancient saying from the East that addresses the triumph of Self over ego. It goes, "All things, good and bad, crumble into dust before the oncoming feet of the Lord." If we try to replace "bad" with "good" we must first determine what is good and what is bad. Then we must figure out what has to be done to replace bad with good. These are decisions that cannot be made by the limited human mind. Yet ego has convinced us otherwise. Pure observation removes us from the "playing God" game and allows us to watch as creation effortlessly unfolds. When we stop trying to fix what is, we are free to observe life as it is. While watching what is, we lose interest in what could be or what has been. Suffering then slides quietly beyond our grasp.

Give me my suffering

As you learn to value observing you will immediately sense when ego has snuck back into the game. The contrast is very evident. With ego enters effort. One sure symptom that ego is pulling your strings is when living becomes an effort. You become focused on some goal and generate enormous exertion to reach your goal. Effort is friction caused by a sense of duality. You have the perception that you are pitted against some object or person or idea or situation. It becomes "me" against the impediments to my goal. This is a heavy burden indeed. This perception that life somehow presents you with obstacles to be overcome so you can better control circumstances is dangerous. This perception causes problems, and then in turn thrives on them. This perception thrives on problems.

When we do not know Self, "me" has no sense of wholeness. Without the anchor of awareness to secure it to the unmoving Self, "me" is buffeted by the waves of chance and happenstance. Little "me" is repeatedly dashed on the rocky shores of relativity and it loves it. "Take your best shot," "me" screams above the tumult of torment. "Give me my suffering." Does this sound absurd to you? Is your mind calmly telling you that no one would choose to suffer? Maybe we should take a closer look at the motivation of "me."

Do you know someone who loves his problems? Do you know people who thrive on crisis, whose life is an honest-to-goodness soap opera? Peace becomes their enemy and they fight against every solution to their problems. These are the kinds of people about whom you find yourself saying, "Don't they ever learn? They keep making the same mistake over and over again." Their sense of who they are is inseparably entangled with turmoil. They don't listen to reason. If they would just listen to you, you could tell them how to rise above their suffering. But could you? Are you so different from them?

I don't know the answer to that last question. Maybe you don't either. But you have to ask it of yourself. Are you making the same basic perceptual mistake as a person who needs emotional pain to bring meaning into his life? Is your life different only because you rely on family, money, politics or religion to give you a sense of purpose and meaning?

Life is like a long car ride

Life is like a long car ride. We go merrily along on our way not paying much attention to this or that. Our conscious mind, flitting aimlessly like a butterfly from topic to topic, has no apparent use on this trip because the sub-conscious mind seems to know the way. The conscious mind, being conscious, soon asks itself, "What is the meaning of this trip?" If it says, "To arrive at my destination." then the conscious mind can continue to let life flow by, routinely unobserved, because driving down the road of life can be accomplished mostly on auto-pilot. Pretty soon it begins to feel bored and starts to invent games like children do on long car rides. The games help pass the time. They can be competitive like whoever sees the first red Corvette wins. Or they can work together against time. They could help each other spot 10 Michigan license plates before the next rest area. This is probably not a particularly difficult task if you happen to be driving in Michigan, but that is not the point. Here is the point: All games are against something. It may be "me" against them or "me" and them against it, but no matter what game is being played "me" is always doing battle.

If the mind is not engaged in games it will create them. It does not like to be bored. To some people boredom is worse than death. They may play life-threatening games that make them "feel" more alive. Unfortunately for them a kind of mental callus forms. In order to feel ever more alive they must increase the level of danger so it can be felt through that callus. Paradoxically the effort to feel more alive many times ends in their totally "non-feeling" physical death.

No matter how it chooses to do it, the bored mind must strive for greater and greater accomplishment. The mental callus forms in all such minds no matter what the game. If your game is money you must always have more. If it is power or lust, you must have more and more. If you do good deeds you must perform greater goodness to feel alive. To cope with the pain of a meaningless existence we become "feeling" addicts. We are addicted to the game.

The mental callus is actually a good thing. If it did not form we would be satisfied playing the same simple game over and over until the end of the trip. And that would be the greatest loss of all. Sooner or later we have to ask why a callus forms in the first place. In this case, it is there to tell you that the games you are playing are not the reason for the journey. The callus makes it harder and harder for you to ignore the real reason. At some time, somewhere along the way you must ask, "What more is there to life?" Many of you may have already asked that question and then chosen a different game to play as your solution. You looked at the two options, boredom and game playing, and decided that you were not playing the right game. But there is a third option. And this option dissolves the disharmony of the dualistic perception of "me" against the world.

The third option does not make sense to ego-oriented minds and thus it is discarded as having no real value. In actuality, the third option is the only option we can choose if we want to live in peace. I am sure you are way ahead of me at this point. The third option open to us on this long car ride is the option to innerthink, to pay attention with complete awareness. To what do we pay attention? To whatever life offers us, to whatever is. Whether it is raining, sunny, hot or freezing, we observe that. If we are cruising along the expressway or locked bumper-to-bumper in rush-hour traffic we remain aware. When day yields to night, and night back into day, we observe that, too. We listen to the conversation of the other passengers and feel the car swaying and bumping down the road of life. We need nothing more than to be present.

To an outsider unfamiliar with innerthinking, that might seem boring. But she would be wrong. In truth, boredom is a dead giveaway that you have stopped innerthinking. If you are not innerthinking and you are not playing a game, you are bored. Boredom is your wake-up call. When life is not very interesting and you feel a little restless you should find yourself saying, "Oh, I've stopped innerthinking." And get right back to observing the trip.

When we pay attention to what is taking place on our long car ride, something hidden is revealed. At first, a pleasant stillness settles over us. As we continue innerthinking, that stillness grows into peace, then joy, bliss and finally ecstasy. Eu-feelings are the symptom of innerthinking. When their presence is appreciated it slowly begins to dawn on us that we don't have to win a game to be happy. And we don't have to get to the end of the trip to feel like a winner, to feel complete. Here we are right in the middle of our journey through life and for no apparent reason at all we are at peace, which automatically completes us.

After realizing wholeness you may ask yourself, "If I am already whole then what value do the circumstances of life have?" And then like a bolt from the blue you understand, not with the mind but an unmistakable "knowing" that emanates from everywhere at once. You come to know that you are the game. Along with this insight you realize one thing more. You are also the Game Master. Out of you the game is created. You are both creator and player. When you only know yourself as a player you forsake your greater status. The instant your awareness opens to accommodate your role as Game Master the game for you is over. You have won and your prize is nothing. Your honest and consistent attention was all that was needed. You gave up your toys in favor of what is.

Nothing really changes. Life continues to bump along, carrying you along with it. But you are changed. You have a foot in two worlds now, the mundane and the divine. The mundane life of potholes and traffic snarls coexists with the divine knowing that all is just as it should be.

Fear is afraid of dying

The end of the long car ride is just another opportunity to be present. There is no fear of death in the present. This is your experience and mine as well. If you doubt what I am saying then put it to the test right now.

Do a session of Mood Melting (Experience Five) thinking about death. Start with the death of something you are not emotionally attached to like a flower or an animal or even a season like summer. In subsequent sessions increase your emotional attachments by observing pets and people close to you. Observe your emotions closely. Finally observe your own death. If you encounter strong emotions then do short sessions with longer periods between them. This is very similar to a Tibetan Buddhist technique used to help aspirants to come to know their Self.

Please do not get confused. The feelings you have while you are acutely aware are uncomfortable but they can not cause you to suffer. The experience is more like watching a movie. You are a detached witness. The movies playing out on the screen of your mind are old films taken when you were not paying attention. When your mind was otherwise involved these events took up residence in your memory. Watching them now with natural detachment allows you to effortlessly experience the difference between your Self and your controlling memories. You are not your emotions. You are not your thoughts. You are beyond the reach of both. You are pure stillness and peace and unbounded compassion. Yes, you are. If you doubt this then you must take more time to get to know your Self.

It is fear that is afraid of dying. Ego is fear. The fear of death you feel, is actually ego's irrational fear of losing its identity when merging with Self. The death of psychological time is the death of fear. Innerthinking kills time and fear and ego in one slash of the sword of awareness. It amazes me how easily it all goes away as soon as I begin to observe. Every time we pay attention to the here and now we kill suffering. Now how incredible is that? Without effort, suffering dies a swift death. There is nothing more to it. We have all we need at this exact moment to end suffering, not only for ourselves but for all of humanity. It is absolutely imperative that we wake up now.

If we have whiled away our time playing games along the way, then when we arrive at our destination we will have only our memories. If they are generally good then we tell ourselves that we had a good life. True enough, we may have collected many friends, much money and fame, but don't you consider those things a measure of how good your life was? They are not really yours, are they? You just think you own them. Like an amoeba, ego engulfs them and assimilates them to nourish its fantasy of "me." At the end of your long car ride your possessions and even your memories drift beyond the ego's grasp to merge with the forgotten. As death's eternal cold seeps through the body and into your mind, you will have one last chance to remember your Self. Your story will be reflected in your eyes. At that tender moment just before passing, will we see confusion, the fear of the unknown? Or will the deep secret of the Self reflect through your eyes like the glint of the morning sun from a peaceful pool?

When Besso, a life-long friend of Einstein's died, Einstein wrote in a letter to Besso's sister:

> ...And now he has preceded me briefly in bidding farewell to this strange world. This signifies nothing. For us believing physicists the distinction between past, present, and future is only an illusion, even if a stubborn one.

I do not know what happens to individual consciousness after the body dies. I used to think about it a lot at one point in my life. It was important because I didn't want to lose what I had, my family, my position in the community, my youth and everything else my mind owned. Since I have been dying to fear every day I no longer fear death. I used to be motivated to keep my body in shape because I was afraid not to. I wanted to live a long time. I was suffering in every aspect of my life and I wanted more time to get things right. That thinking is not only misguided, it is mad. Time was the very thing that was causing the pain. See how clever ego is. It has us craving the very things that are causing the sickness. Time is a true addiction. Now I take care of my body, and everything else that needs my care, because it is natural to do so. Just like it is natural for water to run downhill or a flower to open to the sun. I am certain that if I contracted a terminal disease today that I would initially experience great fear. I would struggle on some level with my own mortality. But because I have reached momentum, the fear of death would automatically trigger a deeper more profound peace born of my heightened attention. I would perceive death as the natural process that it is. It would not become a source of abhorrent behavior growing out of fear. It would be observed as a natural progression of life like the falling of fruit from the bough.

Problems are the games we play

Some might say that their problems are not games. "My problems," they announce with some pride, "are not child's play. They are serious and sometimes even life-threatening." Who could argue with that statement? The problems inherent in humankind are very serious. At no other time in history have we had the means to totally eliminate our species from this lush nurturing planet. A club in the hand of ancient man might end 10 or 15 lives on a good day. A button under the finger of contemporary man could end all life, except for maybe the most adaptable bacteria. "...and the meek shall inherit the earth."

Global problems are born from the individual mind, that is, the individual suffering mind. Problems are the games we play. They make us pay attention. Problems make us feel alive. If you ask a free climber why she does it she'll say because it makes her feel alive. What does that mean? It means that rock climbing makes her pay attention to what she is doing. When her fingers strain to find a grip in a single crack in a cliff face a thousand feet above the rocks below, she is paying attention. If her mind is on her promotion at work or a failing relationship, she may miss a foothold and spiral downward into oblivion. (By the way, this is the only way that autothinking ends suffering.) Rock climbing forces her to observe. So do other sports, getting a raise and driving recklessly in traffic. The problem is that when we do something that makes us pay attention we credit the activity for generating the feeling of wholeness. In reality it is innerthinking, paying attention while activity is playing itself out, that provides the sense of aliveness.

It is the problem that makes us pay attention but *it is the attention that spawns eu-feelings*. That is why most of us create problems. They make us feel alive. And in order to keep the illusion intact, ego convinces us that we really don't create our problems. We believe that they come from somewhere "out there." We are convinced that other people or circumstances, organizations or governments are responsible for our suffering. Or we may think that some broken part of our mind is responsible and that we can fix if we can only use our mind the right way. Never happen. It never has and it never will.

Let's get back into the car and continue our long car ride. This time you are the driver. You are getting bored and maybe a little sleepy. Your mind drifts off to the future/past and you are autothinking when the car in front of you suddenly stops. Instantly your mind is back in the present. You didn't have to tell yourself to come back, apply the break and take evasive measures. It just happened. You did the right thing at the right time when you became present. If your mind had still been autothinking you would have been unaware of any change in driving conditions and not been able to take the necessary measures to avert the danger. So not only does innerthinking eliminate suffering by bringing wholeness to activity, it also takes care of you while you are present. Even if you hit the car in front of you, you are not suffering when it happens. It is only afterwards, when ego regains control, that we begin to suffer. It is after the initial trauma, when our past and future can be reviewed by the mind, that we feel fear, self-pity and anger.

Innerthinking produces an undercurrent of peace and protection. All we need do to receive this blessing is pay attention. But this is not what we normally do. We are driving on autopilot, waking up only long enough to avoid running off the road before slipping back into the seductive slumber of future/past. We feel alive only when something rouses us from our stupor. If we don't want to invest the effort it takes to become a mountain climber, not to worry. We still have our problems, the lazy man's way to feel alive. Somewhere in the far reaches of our minds we feel a dissatisfaction that gnaws incessantly at the edges of our consciousness. We learn to quiet the dissatisfaction by creating problems that make us feel alive. We create problems to alleviate the pain of alienation. In our car analogy that is akin to leaving the road and driving cross country. Our world may be more interesting and even dangerous, but at least we are not bored. There is a way to stay on the highway and not be bored. When we pay attention, everything begins to fit into its place. Life enfolds us in its freshness and vibrancy and we feel complete. When we awaken to the now, we feel alive no matter what our condition or surroundings dictate.

Why is a joke funny?

Some years ago I was giving a talk on Unity Consciousness at an international convention for the Coptic Fellowship. Seated before me were spiritual seekers from many exotic places. Somewhere in the middle of the presentation I had become bogged down in theory and lost the spirit of the topic. Neither I nor my hopeful audience was feeling much unity. I decided to shift gears. I began to tell them a story about how we are fundamentally of the same essence. I told them that we are all one. By way of illustration, I pointed out that it wouldn't matter if we were the Dalai Lama or a hotdog vendor. There is no basic difference between the two. "In fact," I told them, "if you could spend one day with the Dalai Lama, and one day with a hotdog vendor you would find that people coming to them would be asking for the same thing. You would hear them say, "Make me one with everything."

After the initial laughter quieted someone in the audience suggested that I was the "hotdog" and the laughter erupted anew. As the laughter died down for a second time I replied, "That must be why they call me frank." Needless to say returning to the theory of Unity Consciousness was out of the question. At that point it would have been counterproductive anyway. The theory of Unity had then yielded to the experience of Unity.

Have you ever asked yourself why a joke is funny? The mechanics of a joke are the same as the mechanics of a problem. They both create distortions in the mundane. Problems and jokes distort our sense of normalcy. The distortion from a joke creates enough discomfort to momentarily free us from the fetters of autothink.

Here's how it works. As the joke is being told we begin to pay closer attention. Have you noticed how quiet and focused someone becomes when they are listening to a joke? Attention reflects in the mind as a mild eu-feeling, like stillness and the joy of anticipation. As this happens, we begin to feel relief from the quiet desperation that permeates the constantly autothinking mind. Then the punch line is delivered. Here the greatest distortion is experienced just before the mind "gets it." You can actually see some people looking, waiting for all the pieces to fall into place. This is the time of no-mind. When the flash of insight illumines the mind there is a sense of relief as order is reestablished and attention is deepened. The sudden release from this kind of twisted chaos causes laughter, a buoyant reaction in the mind and body as Self regains the throne momentarily vacated by ego.

We mistakenly credit the conditions of the joke for the explosion of gaiety that comes with the laughter. The good feeling actually comes from the gap between the joke and the laughter. Pay attention the next time you laugh at a joke. You will notice a space or gap in your thinking just before you laugh. That silence is the source of the feelings of gladness and mirth. It is the contrast between the bizarre composition of the joke followed by the complete order in silence that causes the spontaneous outburst we call laughter.

This is what happens when a Zen master asks a student to reflect upon an unanswerable question, or koan, like "What is the sound of one hand clapping?" or "What is the color of the wind?" The koan does not seem to make sense and the student must examine it closely. The mind is made to analyze, or at least rationalize. That is what it does. It works very hard to find the answer. It is only when the mind gives up that the solution dawns. This increased attention brings with it an ordered stillness which is the object of the exercise. Before the student "gets" the punch line, his mind is in the gap reflecting pure awareness. This then inspires a flash of spiritual insight, or satori. In the case of a joke, the release from the twisted tension to the realization of our still and ordered Self occurs quickly just after the punch line. So great is that distortion that we laugh when order is reestablished.

This does not mean that you will not find jokes funny when you are innerthinking. Jokes are still funny, but not in the same way. A joke arouses a kind of cosmic laughter that is at the same time local and universal. Peace is surprised by joy. The Jokester is surprised by His own creation.

A line drawn in air

As you spend more time with your Self, psychological pain grows fainter and less repressive. By way of explanation, let's say that you have come by a machine that can increase present awareness of Self. As you turn the knob it increases the intensity of presence. As presence intensifies the first thing you will notice is a sense of well-being. As it gets stronger well-being expands to a kind of knowing that everything is just right as it is. You intuit that your life, all life is perfect. There is nowhere you need to go, and nothing you need to fix. As you look around you notice an apparent contradiction. Everything is individually alive with its own uniqueness and at the same time a harmonious part of the whole. You see this contradiction as a vibrant, three-dimensional flatness. You feel as if you could stand on your toes and touch the stars with your fingertips. At this point, presence has become so strong that it begins to dominate what your senses perceive. It is like being in very bright sunlight. The sunlight is brighter than the objects you are looking at. Except this light emanates from within the objects rather than being reflected by them. Simultaneously, awareness of inner presence becomes so strong that your attention is first and foremost on that. Your thoughts and emotions are secondary in impact and importance. You feel nurtured and protected by a force that is no different than your very Self. This experience ends addiction and struggle and suffering. This is the end of psychological pain.

Psychological pain dims because of a weakening of the impulse that creates desire. When presence is absent impulses make a strong impression on the mind. You may see a red sports car that you desire so much, you alter your whole life in order to obtain it. You may even create a considerable inconvenience for yourself and others in the process. But it seems that you have no choice. The impulse that created the desire is very strong. If you are not observing, then you are at the mercy of your desires.

Practicing presence washes away old desires and keeps new ones from forming. In the East it is said that an impulse made in the mind empty of presence is like chiseling a line in granite. As the mind starts to fill with presence the impact of a desire is less. It is more like a line drawn in the sand. It is easier to erase a desire drawn in sand than one in granite. Greater presence in mind is like drawing a line in water. And finally, in a mind full of presence, desires become like lines drawn in the air. Psychological pain passes almost unnoticed.

MAIN POINTS FOR CHAPTER ELEVEN

Overcoming Psychological Pain

- Fear underlies all other emotions. When fear dissolves it is replaced by an unconditional eu-feeling like peace or joy or love.

- You cannot fight fear with fear and get peace.

- Observing Self overshadows the fear of death.

- Time is an addiction.

- More time, living longer, will not alleviate fear. Ego has us craving the very thing that is causing our fear.

- It is attention that makes us feel alive, not the problem or the activity.

- Problems are the games we play. They make us pay attention.

- Problems, jokes and Zen koans are similar in that they distort our sense of normalcy, creating heightened awareness.

- As presence grows in our awareness, psychological pain diminishes and eventually becomes impotent.

CHAPTER 12
Overcoming Physical Pain

"The art of inner-body awareness will develop into a completely new way of living, a state of permanent connectedness with Being, and will add a depth to your life that you have never known before."

Eckhart Tolle

Fantastic voyage

Some years ago, I think it was sometime in the 60's I saw a movie called "Fantastic Voyage" written by Isaac Asimov. It was a great flight of fantasy into the human body. A submarine and its crew were shrunk to almost microscopic size and injected into the blood stream of a human suffering from an inoperable blood clot in the brain. The idea was for the miniaturized submarine and crew to travel through the blood to the brain and dissolve the life-threatening blood clot. They had to do this before the miniaturization process wore off and they expanded back to normal size. They wouldn't want to do that while still inside the patient. Not a pretty picture. I won't ruin the ending for those of you who may want to read the book or dig up an old copy of the video, but Asimov tapped into the natural curiosity we all have for what goes on inside the body. A submarine and crew is an ingenious way to lead our awareness into our bodies. I felt a sense of awe as the crew was swept along the arterial highway and observed firsthand the majesty that is our body.

The human body can elicit a powerful fascination. That fascination can be so strong as to create a fixation. A fixation on the body can take many forms, like vanity and narcissism or fear of illness and aging. Fixations of any kind nurture "me" and starve "I." When you identify with your body, your suffering will increase and your body will age more rapidly. Aging becomes a lifelong injury instead of a natural blossoming of Self expression. You perceive that when your body is injured, you are injured. When your body is injured it changes your perception of who you are. Over the period of your life the body-fixated mind has quantified physical damage. For instance, if you identify with your body you might feel that a cut finger gives you permission to get angry or receive a little sympathy. A broken finger entitles you to more sympathy and possibly more anger if the circumstances support it. An amputated finger gives you the right to lifelong sympathy and an option to be angry at the world for the harm it unjustly inflicted on you.

In many spiritual disciplines the body is the enemy. It is seen as a hindrance to spiritual growth and an object of disgust. Some disciplines actually inflict injury on the body in an effort to free the mind from its attachment to the flesh. Denying the body is merely a negative attachment. It does not matter whether you have an attachment or an aversion to the body, neither will lead you to the unchangeable, untouchable Self.

Your body can be your prison, your concrete cellblock. Or it can be the "wind beneath your wings." Your body like your mind is a wonderful expression of Self. It is an easily opened gateway to peace. Let's take a closer look at your body. Let's take our own fantastic voyage.

Mind and body—Hand in glove

Earlier we went through the different levels of mind, thinking, feeling and security to find I Am, the basic "stuff " of the mind. Your body also has levels that lead to the same end, I Am. When "I am body" and "I am mind" finally fall away, they leave us observing pure I Am. Experience One demonstrated this process in the mind. Shortly we will experience a similar process by using the body.

For our own fantastic voyage, we will go not through the body but into it, layer by layer. What do you suppose is the final layer of the body? Let's find out.

All of us are familiar with the gross aspects of our bodies. Most obvious is the skin, hair, eyes, mouth, hands and feet and the like. What goes on under the skin is a bit more of a mystery. We know from medical scientists that we have organs, soft tissue, bones, nerves, blood and so on. Moving deeper into the body we can see the cells that make up these structures. There are also symbiotic organisms along with harmful bacteria and viruses apparent at this level. Inside the cell we see mitochondria, DNA, etc., and within them we begin to see chemical reactions taking place at the molecular level. Past the molecules we find atoms subatomic particles and waves and finally I Am, undifferentiated Self.

The last layers of the body are the same as the mind! The body passes through the mind on its way to becoming physical. The mind begins at the level of the subtlest wave created. As the wave's frequency slows down it becomes "heavier." The mind is differentiated from matter, and particularly the body, by the frequency of its vibration. A good way to look at the body is as solidified mind. This is an oversimplified statement to be sure but it will serve our purposes here just fine.

By the way, do not confuse mind with brain. Brain is a physical structure housed in the cranium. Mind has only the limitations that the mind puts on it. If you think your mind is in your brain then that is where you will find it. Mind is not subject to the physical laws. However, you can assign it limitations and it will act within those restraints like a well-trained dog.

Mind fits in body like a hand in a glove. When you wiggle the fingers of your hand, the fingers of your glove will also wiggle. What the mind experiences the body will experience. A thought in the mind immediately creates a neuropeptide in the body. A neuropeptide is a molecule that triggers additional chemical and physical reactions in the body. This is quite amazing when you think about it. Here is a concrete example of mind creating matter! And it is taking place between your mind and body right now.

While the creation of a neuropeptide is immediate, other physical changes stimulated by your mind can take days and months and years to manifest in your body. And the mental commands have to be repeated over and over again to etch their gross effects into your physiology. These are the mental tapes that keep playing while you are autothinking.

Some systems encourage us to counter the negative tapes with positive ones. But as we found out in the last chapter, we cannot possibly know how deeply or how convoluted the tendrils of any negative behavior can be. Approaching our problems in this way will give rise to the mythological thousand-headed serpent. When you cut off one of its heads two more take its place.

Physical manifestations of mental disharmony abound. Stooped shoulders from carrying the world on your shoulders, ulcers from worry, headaches from tension, asthma from anxiety, eyes that do not meet yours out of shame or dart around the room out of fear, a rigid and locked pelvis from sexual dysfunction are only a few such examples. Ancient and alternative healing systems have associated organs with emotions as a diagnostic tool. In such a system you might find that anger finds its way to the liver, grief the lungs, fear the kidneys, pride the gall bladder, low self-esteem the spleen and sorrow the heart.

There is an old Ayurvedic saying that is particularly poignant today. It suggests that if you want to know what was dominating your mind in the past, look at your body today. If you want to know what your body will be like in the future, look at what you are thinking today. At least 5,000 years ago, and I would wager many thousands of years before that, humans recognized that the mind imprints the body. The question is, "What can we do about it now?" Why innerthink, of course. I might add that it does not matter what was in your mind in the past. Nor need we be concerned about our future if we innerthink today. One of the most powerful gateways to the Self is through the body. The body is a gate that swings in two directions. Inward it opens to the mind and outward into phenomenal creation. In either direction you will find Self and peace. All of creation can be found literally and figuratively at your feet.

The subtle body

The subtle body can be found vibrationally between the mind and the physical body. The subtle body is a matrix of energy patterns for the next level of gross body manifestation. On a vibratory level it is heavier than mind and lighter than the physical body. It is mind taking form as body. The subtle body is actually an infinite number of "energy bodies" that I collectively refer to as the subtle body out of convenience. The infinite levels of the subtle body act as a single body and transmit information between the mind and physical body.

You can actually see the heaver aspects of the subtle body with your physical eyes. If you hold you hand out at arm's length and look at your fingers against a completely white or completely black surface you will see what I am talking about. Focus your eyes on the end of one of your fingers. Give your eyes time to adjust. When they do you will be able to see a thin, clear vibration about 1/16th of an inch beyond the end of your fingertip. If a black background doesn't yield results switch to a white one, or vice versa. Don't be in a hurry. You will see it. Move your hand and the energy interference that is your subtle body will move with it. Once you get used to seeing this thin expression of your subtle body, look a little farther out from your finger. There you will see a wider but fainter band of energy. This is another one of your subtle bodies vibrating at a higher rate. In fact, they go on well beyond your body to infinity.

If you do not at first see your subtle body at the end of your finger don't be dismayed. Your mind may not be attuned to the idea as of yet, but it will happen. Some people can see many expressions of the subtle body, including colors. They can gather a good deal of information about the physical body and the mind by observing these different expressions of the subtle body. You can develop this skill to one degree or another, but it is not at all necessary for you see any more than you already do to be at peace.

It is easy to get carried away by the excitement and mystery of invisible worlds made visible, but they can also be a trap. I know a number of very talented people with astonishing special "powers" who are suffering just as much as the rest of us. If you have a talent you should develop it. You are impelled by the evolutionary forces of nature to find and express your talents. But if you get attached to those talents and miss their purpose you can create great suffering. If you find yourself going for the flash you may want to take a closer look at your underlying motivation. Do not trade purpose for peace.

Anyway, if you want to see the subtle world, including angels and auras and disincarnate teachers, you can make a special set of glasses that have a third lens in the middle and above the two normal lenses. This third lens covers your third "spiritual" eye found in the middle of your forehead. These special glasses correct spiritual myopia. With these special glasses the spiritual world will no longer appear fuzzy and out of focus. I'm kidding, I'm kidding! Do not try this at home. You will only waste your valuable time, much as I have just done.

Finding your subtle body

When I use the phrase "feeling your body" I am referring to feeling your subtle body. It is in the subtle body that we find the pivot point for peace. Opening our awareness to the subtle body creates a wondrously nurturing environment for the physical body. It fosters both healing and growth. It slows down aging and speeds up the infusion of peace in our everyday life. Finding the subtle body starts with our closely observing the physical body.

Experience Six
Finding your subtle body

Find a comfortable position either lying down or sitting. Close your eyes and observe your thoughts. After 10 seconds or so, switch your aware-ness to your right hand. Don't move your hand; just pay close attention to what you feel. Become aware of any sensations in your right hand. Can you feel the blood pulsing, or the tenseness of muscle or tightness of sinew? Is your hand heavy or light? Can you feel a tingling, relax-ation or liveliness in your right hand? Or you may feel a faint electricity or vibration in the cells. Observe closely. This is a general sensation throughout. Quietly pay close attention and it will be there. When you become aware of it, switch your attention to your left hand. Does it feel different, less alive, less vibrant or heavier? Now look for the same general sensation you felt in your right hand to be in your left hand. Then feel that sensation in both hands at the same time. Now pay atten-tion to how your subtle body can be felt in your whole physical body.

The sensation that you feel in your hands is your vibrating subtle body. It can be perceived as lightness, a vibrant energy, tingling, relaxation, warmth, liveliness or any number of other general sensations. General means it will not be localized in one part of the hand like a pulse or an itch. The subtle body is alive with consciousness and energy. You have just awakened your mind to its existence in your body. At once all three, the mind, the physical body and the subtle body, are aligned. Observing your subtle body is like bringing the magnet of Self in contact with the iron filings of mind, body and subtle body. This establishes a harmonizing flow of Self between them. Now healing and growth are accelerated in all three. O.K., let's return to exercise six: Feeling Your Body. Allow yourself twenty uninterrupted minutes to complete it.

Finding your subtle body (continued)

Sit or lie down as before. Become aware of your subtle body in your feet. (Again, you may experience it as tingling, relaxation or liveliness, a faint vibration or electricity or any other generalized feeling.) When you become aware of the energizing presence of your subtle body in your feet, move your awareness to your ankles. Once you feel your subtle body in your ankles become aware of it in your lower legs, knees and upper legs. Just spend 3 or 4 seconds on each area of the body after you feel the subtle body there. Now take your awareness to the pelvic region, lower back, upper back, across the shoulders, the arms, hands and fingers, your sides, your abdomen and then your chest. Then feel your subtle body in your neck, your lips, nose, eyes and ears. Then your forehead, the top (crown) of your head and the back of your head, and then become aware of your subtle body in your whole head. Finally, become aware of your subtle body vibrating within your whole body all at once. Feel your whole body in this way as long as you like. Great healing is taking place so don't be in a hurry. When you are finished take enough time so that your return to activity is not jarring.

You may be feeling any number of things in your body and mind just by becoming aware of your subtle body. If you had some physical discomfort before "feeling your body" it probably disappeared or at least lessened in intensity. You may have felt some mental stress or had been worried about something before "feeling your body" and now find that it has completely dissolved into the subtle body. If nothing else, you will be feeling a deep relaxation in your body, and a very peaceful mind.

Let me remind you that we did not set out to relax the body or reduce mental/emotional stresses. All you did was to become aware of your subtle body in your physical body. That is all. Any physical or mental benefits you realized came naturally from that awareness. Nothing else was needed.

Good deeds can make bad things happen

Do not confuse "feeling your body" with relaxation or meditation techniques. All you did was bring your awareness to your subtle body and the natural harmonizing and healing effect of that direct awareness took over. Actually, this is how relaxation and meditation techniques work. The results do not come from performing a specific task as is normally taught. Results that are realized from any technique come from increased awareness and not from a structured protocol. If you did not bring your awareness to the process then nothing would happen. Once you are aware, then whatever you focus your attention on becomes enlivened.

If you become aware of a negative thing it does not mean that the negativity will grow. In fact, the opposite is true. Infusing negativity with awareness by observing it, without judgment, will actually reduce or eliminate the perceived negativity. It works just like "feeling your body" did on the negative elements in your body and mind. The real harm is done when you interact with negativity without awareness. Without awareness you can create disastrous results even by performing positive actions. If an act is performed without pure awareness then the only result has to be more negativity. Christ told us that we cannot get into Heaven by good deeds alone. It is awareness that heals, not philosophy, ideas, or good intentions by themselves. This is the reason we see so much suffering despite the good intentions and actions of the majority of the world's citizens. They launch their "good deeds" from the platform of the autothinking mind of distracted awareness. Without the wisdom of Self to support their actions, even the best intentions go astray.

During the "feeling your body" exercise, I asked you to become aware of your subtle body. You did not make the subtle body stronger; you just became more aware of it's existence. The subtle body remained unchanged. It was your awareness that became more open to observing the subtle body. As this happened, harmony between mind, body and subtle body increased accordingly. With practice you will be able to "feel your body" with your eyes open while driving in rush hour traffic or having a lively discussion with a friend. Feeling your whole body during activity keeps you anchored in Self. I recommend that you start by sitting and "feeling your body" as often as you comfortably can. If you are short on time you can just feel your whole body and not the parts. Or you can observe the subtle body in larger areas of your physical body. For instance, you could start with your feet, then your legs, your lower torso, upper torso, arms and finish with your head. This shorter version is also very effective. Just remember to end every session by feeling your whole body for two or three minutes.

Feeling your subtle body is best practiced just before you go to sleep and immediately upon waking. What a neat exercise. You don't even have to get out of bed to do it. When you are able to do it with eyes open, do it as often as you remember to. Feel your whole body while driving, talking, reading, singing, eating and at every other time. I do not want to give away the ending, but soon a wonderful change will come over you. It will be a delicious surprise like a cherry in the middle of a piece of chocolate.

Kiss it and make it better

One day I was in the living room watching my 3-year-old son playing with his fire truck and Tonka toy cars, just beyond the patio doors in the backyard. What a blue-eyed, blond haired wonder he was, totally absorbed in Self. Sitting on the ground, he was driving his cars along dirt roads and around rock buildings. It must have been time to put out a fire in one of the rocks for I saw him looking around for his bright red fire truck. When he spied it, he got up quickly, tangled his feet and fell back to earth on his hands and knees. Immediately he grabbed one knee as crocodile tears rolled down both cheeks. I fought the urge to duck into a phone booth to emerge as Superdad and rescue him from the arch-villain Life. I could see his injury was not serious, and I wanted to know how he would handle the intrusion of pain into his peaceful world. Brad looked around to see who was watching, but did not see me. When he saw no one, he managed two quick sobs, grabbed his fire truck and returned to put out the other fire. Fifteen or twenty minutes later he stood up, walked to the door and slid it open. Still not seeing me, he stopped and drank the last of the apple juice he had left on the floor before he went out to play. He carefully set the glass down with two hands and looked up. He saw me watching him. As soon as our eyes met he broke into tears, grabbed his hurt knee with two chubby little hands and cried, "Daddy, I faw down." Ah, the joys of parenthood. I swooped him into my arms and gave him a big hug. Then I sat him on my knee, brushed the dirt from his scratch and kissed it and made it all better.

Pain is not suffering. Pain is physical. Pain does not become suffering until the mind throws emotion into the mix. The emotive force comes from future/past. My son immediately felt pain when he fell. Since the injury was slight and the pain subsided quickly and there was no one nearby with which to share his misfortune, he quietly returned to his play. His pain was forgotten until he saw me some time later. Already, at the innocent age of 3, my son had learned how to "work the crowd" to satisfy his emotional needs. This is cute in a child. It gives a parent an excuse to shower down seven kinds of love on that beautiful soul. On the other hand, suffering by adults is anything but cuddly.

Every trauma is comprised of three different elements. They are the physical, mental/emotional, and chemical. One will be more dominant than the other two but all three will always be involved. It doesn't matter if you have a broken leg or a broken heart, you will find the trauma triad ever present. "How," you say, "is a broken leg emotional or chemical?" "Likewise," you object, "how is a broken heart physical or chemical?" "And what the heck is chemical anyway?"

If you break your leg you have sustained a physical injury. While the physical break is the dominant component of this healing triad of body-mind-chemistry, healing can only be complete if the chemistry and mind components are also addressed. The bone will "set" physically by metabolizing or mobilizing nutrients (chemicals) like calcium to rebuild the break and reestablish the integrity of the bone. Inflammation is a chemical reaction that creates heat at the site of injury. Reducing inflammation will reduce pain and encourage healing both physically and mentally. Most often forgotten with a physical injury is the emotional trauma it produces, however small. It has probably been forgotten because most physicians don't think it is important. They don't understand why it is necessary to help a patient heal emotionally from a physical trauma.

There are a number of disciplines that recognize the value of treating the emotional element of the healing triad. Several chiropractic techniques address the emotional component. I attended a seminar on one such technique in Chicago in the early 90"s. The doctor who had developed it asked if anyone in the room had physical injuries that would not heal despite traditional physical and nutritional therapies. Several of us raised our hands and I was chosen to be the guinea pig. I explained that I had a shoulder pain that had been getting progressively worse over the past few years and I was not aware of any specific injury that may have caused it. The doctor asked me to show him where the pain was and how it restricted the movement of my arm and shoulder. His diagnosis determined that there was an emotional component to the injury that had not been addressed. He also suggested that it was a strong emotion, probably a love-hate relationship, and probably when I was a young man. Indeed, I had met and fallen madly in love with a redheaded beauty in my late teens. It was my first serious experience with the vortex of emotions swirling around conditional love. I could not remember a specific injury from that time in my life, but I was very athletic and could have injured it in any number of ways. I had not thought much about it. The doctor then proceeded to make an "emotional" adjustment. Then he asked me to once again put my arm through the offending ranges of motion. A murmur rippled through the observing doctors as they watched my arm move freely and without pain in all directions. I also somehow felt lighter emotionally. That specific pain has not returned to this day.

I had not thought about that relationship in many years. The unresolved emotion somehow chose to take up residence in my shoulder. The technique the doctor used was somewhat convoluted, but in essence he made me open my awareness to the problem. The emotional release technique identified the problem and my awareness dissolved it. But remember, don't get lost in technique. Get lost in awareness.

Specific areas of discomfort and pain in the physical body can be eliminated or reduced by simply paying attention to that area. The following exercise will reduce or remove the physical, mental/emotional and chemical components of pain and dis-ease in your body. Before you start, scan your body to find the areas of discomfort or pain. Also note how you feel emotionally about those specific areas, and your physical condition in general. Grade your physical discomfort from one to ten, ten being unbearable pain. Now, let's get started.

<u>Experience Seven</u>
How to overcome physical pain

Sit or lie down as you like. Close your eyes and become aware of a general presence in your physical body. This can be felt as a tingling, relaxation, liveliness, a faint vibration, electricity or any other generalized feeling. This generalized feeling is the subtle body. Pay attention to it for a minute or more until your awareness of the subtle body is as strong as it can be at this time. Now, allow your awareness to shift to a specific area of your body where pain or discomfort is presiding. Pay close attention to the pain. What kind of pain is it? Is it sharp, aching, throbbing, dull, shooting, etc.? Where exactly is it? What shape is it? Does it have a color or texture? Does it have an emotion attached to it? What else can you observe about this pain?

Do not interfere with the pain. Just watch it very closely. The pain may get more intense at first. Don't worry. Just continue to be easily open to what you feel. If the pain moves, follow it to its new location and start again. Continue observing your pain until it is gone or you wish to move on to a new area of your body. Before you end your session return to "feeling your body." Feel the subtle body for two to five minutes until you feel quite rested and at peace. This will allow time for pain that began to dissolve to gently work its way out of your body. Quietly open your eyes and slowly return to normal activity.

Before you return to activity, while you still have your eyes closed, you may want to re-visit the original area of physical pain or discomfort and grade it as you did before. Your pain will have dissolved or significantly diminished. In addition, your body will feel more fluid and energetic and you will generally feel lighter emotionally. Sometimes you may feel more pain for awhile. This is an indication that deep repair is taking place. In these instances it is good to "feel your body" for a little longer at the end of the session. The increased pain will dissolve naturally at this time or as you go about your normal activities. You can quicken the release of the pain in that area by easily allowing your attention to be on it.

As you research "feeling your body" you will notice that your subtle body is not entrapped within your physical body. Soon you will feel your subtle body outside your physical body. Then you will find that your subtle body fills the whole room. If you step out of doors it will fill the sky. In time, as your awareness refines and expands, you will come to know the whole of creation as your subtle body. The further away from your physical body you are aware of your subtle body, the subtler it will be. Finally, you will watch your subtle body melt into the limitless, unbounded awareness of Self beyond all things. Then no matter what your senses perceive they will also perceive Self. Whatever you think or feel will float on the silent ocean of Self. You have discovered Self in the stillness that permeates the mind and is beyond things. You have discovered that within and beyond all things and thoughts, beyond even the possibility of suffering, you are Self.

The spiritual scientist

As the more rigid Newtonian constructs dissolve into the fluid, ever-vacillating probabilities of quantum physics, so the stilted medical model of the body as a machine will melt into the river of non-changing change. Your body only appears solid. Quantum physicists tell us that like a galaxy, our bodies are mostly space. Even the solid parts are not really solid. They are flickering in and out of existence so rapidly as to appear solid. In actuality, the physical body is frozen thought. And thought, as we have already discovered, is liquid light, sunbeams of the Self. Candice Pert, a Harvard medical scientist and a pioneer in body-mind research has added significant momentum to the demise of this rigid medical model. She stated, *"I can no longer make a strong distinction between the brain and the body.... the research findings...indicate that we need to start thinking about how consciousness can be projected into various parts of the body."* We do not need a fully equipped medical laboratory to reveal the Soul within the body. As spiritual scientists we were born with everything we need. The innerthinking mind is the laboratory. The exercises written within these pages are the experiments. In the history of humankind there has never been so urgent a need to understand that knowledge is structured in Self. Without knowledge of Self all other knowledge is baseless and dangerous. "Know thy Self " is the rallying cry of the spiritual scientist. The pursuit of the corporal sciences has added many wonders to our lives but not one has removed the source of fear and suffering. That is because permanent peace can only be grasped by letting go. The science of Self is the practice of subtraction. It is the reduction of all things to their simplest, most powerful expression. The Self is known by negation. When everything that is not Self is removed then only Self remains. But there is a final discovery to be made. It is this cognition: Self is also mind and body and the phenomenal world. When inner Self and outer Self unite, fear and suffering give way to unshakable peace, and ultimately immortality.

MAIN POINTS FOR CHAPTER TWELVE
Overcoming Physiological Pain

- When you mistake the body for your Self, aging becomes a lifelong injury.

- Your body is a wonderful expression of Self and an easily opened gateway to peace.

- The body is a gate that swings in two directions. Inward it opens to the mind and outward into the phenomenal world.

- The subtle body, connecting the mind and physical body, is a matrix of energy patterns for the physical body and the pivot point for finding inner peace.

- Opening our awareness to our subtle body slows down aging and speeds up the infusion of inner peace. It accelerates healing and growth in the body, mind and subtle body.

- Finding the subtle body starts with closely observing the physical body.

- You can create disastrous results even by performing positive actions, if you do them without Self-awareness.

- Pain is not suffering. Pain is physical, suffering is emotional.

- Every trauma is comprised of three different elements, the physical, mental/emotional and chemical.

CHAPTER 13
The Perfect Relationship

Draw if thou canst the mystic line. Severing rightly His from thine,
which is human, which divine.
Ralph Waldo Emerson

One man's perfect is another man's pain

Relationships come in an infinite variety of sizes, styles and shapes. There's your garden-variety male-female relationship, parent-child, teacher-student and the like. Humans communicate with animals and even with the wind, the waves, forests and mountains. We are fascinated by the notion of invisible beings sharing our space at higher or lower frequencies—the pixies, the specters and angels. Then there is the highest and most invisible being, God.

If it is the parts that define a relationship then it is communication that determines its quality. Communication is the glue that binds the pieces giving rise to a whole greater than its parts. We use many different modes of communication including art, music, sign language, body language, even smoke signals. The mode is the "how" of communication. Content is the heart. If how we communicate were a car then content would be the driver. While the kind of car we drive is important, the driver is the reason the car exists to begin with. So what we share with others is paramount. But let's not stop there for there is more to content than meets the eye.

Within each of us content manifests as a writhing bundle of emotions, thoughts and ideas plus hopes and fears anxious to be expressed. They come from our past and our future to influence how we think and feel now. Many are misled into thinking that their content is who they are. Those who do will never be able to share with another who they really are behind the whirring world of the mind. Their relationships will be sentenced to superficiality, doomed before they begin. If the driver of the car is asleep, what are the chances she will arrive at her destination? And here we come to the secret of the successful relationship. *The quality of our content is directly influenced by the quality of our awareness.*

Awareness changes content, not by making it into something else but by taking something away. Awareness robs content of its solidity and seriousness. It lights it from within, bringing wholeness to the pieces. When Self-aware, we remain the same person and at the same time become brighter and lighter and more human. Our awareness grounds us and gives meaning to our sharing.

It is vital that you grasp this point if you want your relationships to germinate and grow. The quality of your awareness critically impacts the quality of your relationship. And more than that, no two points of individual awareness are the same. Have you ever spoken with another person and come to complete agreement on an issue only to find sometime later that his or her understanding was light years away from yours? Your two points of view differed so drastically that you wonder if you hadn't originally spoken with a double from a parallel universe. Why is that? How does that happen? It begins with awareness.

Miscommunication is an example of the divergence of two points of awareness. This is not the exception but rather the rule, and the rule is absolute. Belief in a fixed or "right" point of view is the germ of destruction that has been passed down through the generations. No two people can ever have the same point of view no matter what they feel or how hard they work at it. Einstein put it this way, "There is no such thing as a simultaneous event." I like to say, "One man's perfect is another man's pain."

Perfection is the product of perception

If it is true that one man's perfect is another man's pain then perfection is a product of perception. And perception is affected by our level of conscious awareness, our ability to observe clearly the perfection of this moment. That means that there are an infinite number of perceptions of perfection, as many as there are perceivers. So, what to do?

Do you remember back in Chapter Two when I mentioned the two simple rules that I use to guide my life? Whenever I feel things are "going wrong" I revisit these two simple axioms for greater awareness. They are 1) life is ultimately harmonious and 2) things are not as I see them. Taking the negative stance we could say that if things are not making sense (rule 1) then it is my perception (rule 2) that needs adjusting. The first thing this does is put all apparent problems where they belong, squarely on my shoulders. I stop blaming other circumstances or people for my pain. I can't even blame my self for my suffering. Basically, all problems are then reduced to a distorted perception of what is. The second thing that this understanding affords us is a definition of perfection that embraces all individual definitions.

When the conditional love relationship hits on hard times the most common perspective is that the other person is not performing up to our expectations. When money is the issue then our partner either doesn't make enough money or spends too much, or both. If we are feeling emotionally deprived then we feel it is our partners who are the cause. They are too distant, demanding or needy. A second common perspective on the failure of a relationship is that we are the cause of disharmony. We might blame ourselves for being emotionally, mentally, physically, socially or even financially at fault. But it really doesn't matter who's at fault, or why. We can brush all that aside. That's right. Go ahead, just let all that nonsense slip away. Finding fault and trying to fix it only creates more fault. The "fix." if you haven't already figured it out, is to realize that there is nothing to fix.

It is impossible to stay in love

What we are asking is, "Is it possible to have a problem-free relationship?" The answer is, "Of course, as soon as we remove the problem." The "problem" as you already know is the mind's perception of the relationship. Your mind creates an image of what you are from memory. Relying on memory for our sense of "me." we divide the world into friend and foe, into things that can help "me" and things that are a threat to maintaining the image of "me."

When we "fall in love"it is "me"that does the falling."I"is always in Love. In the moment, "I" has no need to analyze or to protect Itself. But "me" is always jostling for the upper hand. So when "me" meets she or he, "me" starts ticking off the pros and cons of a possible alliance. Can this person give me what I need? Will he or she hurt me? Remember, what "me" sees is filtered through outdated memory. After the tally is complete, which may take only seconds, "me" proclaims yea or nay. Or it may decide to stay judgment until more data can be accumulated.

Does this seem a little stilted and devoid of humanness? We may feel that meeting someone new is effortless and we either like them or we don't. "We don't keep a score card,"you say, "of good points and bad."Of course that is the way it looks at normal speed. But if we had a mental remote with a slow forward button we could examine our inner mental workings more closely.

Impressions and sensations take place at the speed of light. If we are not paying attention they will run away with us. This is exactly what happens when we fall in love.

Falling in love is a tornado of emotions that lifts us off this ordinary earth to land us lightly in heaven. Through our love we perceive a perfect partner. Everything they do is perfect. Those things and people that upset us before, like a boorish boss, cold coffee or a longwinded neighbor, all pale in the bright light of love. We walk in the clouds for days or even months. But sooner or later we fall back to earth. Why? Why? Why does it always happen that way? No matter how long the relationship lasts we never recapture the sheer power of first days of love.

We can't capture love's intensity for long because we have not earned it. When "me" falls in love it gets a taste of the banquet that "I" enjoys every day. The difference is that there is no single object of affection, no thing that is responsible for the love of "I." "I" loves all things, without reason, without exception. And therein lies the difference. "I" loves without reason and "me" looks for reasons to love. Reasons for loving are born of ego-manipulated mind and subject to its futile pursuit of perfection.

Sooner or later our mate's mask of perfection begins to show signs of wear. Like the theater masks of comedy and tragedy, our smile slowly slumps into a frown. In all likelihood we think that they are responsible for us losing love. We still love them but not like before. Our love takes on more of an intellectual flavor. We may even catch ourselves mentally making a list of the good things about our partner in an effort to persuade ourselves that we still love as much as we always have. A later list may drop any pretense of positive qualities in favor of more negative behaviors. In time, we yield to the reality that the "thrill is gone" and settle into quiet complacency. Or we may actively aggravate our partner in a subconscious effort to relieve our pain. There have been thousands of books written on how to keep your love alive. The truth is it never had a chance to begin with.

When we accept the image of ourselves that is generated by ego we separate ourselves from what we perceive as other images. The image "me" interacts with the image "you." Everything is great as long as the image "you" supports the image "me." Bohm taught us that even the image of "you" is created by "me."

I do not see you as you really are. I see you as my mind wants to see you. You are perceived by "me" as filtered through my ego-influenced mind. That is how "you" is created by "me." Who you really are is a mystery. It has nothing to do with the image I have created and call "you." While I was creating an image of "you", you were busy creating an image of me. We are like two puppeteers each working our own puppet. So engrossed are we in making the puppets interact we never take time to see who is actually pulling the strings of the other puppet.

Krishnamurti revealed that when you have an image of yourself you create a division between yourself and another. He told us that relationships are created between two images that thought has created. He further revealed that the two images have their own needs and desires. They have their own agendas and live virtually isolated taking comfort in the illusion of agreement. Krishnamurti said. "...the images run parallel, like two railway lines, never meeting, except perhaps in bed...What a tragedy it has become." And then, he asks a poignant and most powerful question "Is thought love?"

Thought is love, conditional love. Thought is love never-lasting. Thought, born of the autothinking mind, created "me" and dictates the conditions under which "me" can love. Conditional love is subservient to conditions. Conditions are always changing. Therefore, love is always changing. It can be no other way. You cannot stay in love. It is impossible. Flirting with conditional love is living a lie. You cannot live the illusion of conditional love when Universal Love is only a heartbeat away. Your Self will not allow it.

What is the purpose of relationships?

"Why bother?" you say. Why can't we just stay to ourselves? That's a thought born of struggle and conflict produced when relationships are too much work or pain. While there are a few individuals who are truly at home by themselves, most of us are addicted to the touch, the sound, and the warmth of other human beings. Why is that? Why are we drawn so strongly into interactions with others that ultimately prove hurtful and frustrating?

Think on this question awhile. It is important in coming to know lasting peace. What is the reason for relationships? Why do they exist?

Most of us enter a relationship because we think we will get something out of it. Isn't that so? Depending on the kind of relationship, we may look to realize friendship, protection, money, excitement or danger, intellectual stimulation or physical pleasure. The list is a very long one indeed. The dynamics of the meeting of any two people are unique, never the same. Then, is the purpose of relating with another solely for gain?

Yes! The answer to the question "Why do relationships exist?" is that they do so solely for gain. But they do not exist solely for our selfish gain, quite the contrary. Relationships are not strengthened by more money, control or time. They are not even justified by increasing the intensity of love between two people. Tolle hit it right on the button when he said, "A relationship is to make you aware—not happy." Relationships exist for the sole purpose of waking us up, forcing us to become aware of Self.

If you are looking for a relationship to make you happy or safe or experience love more deeply, forget it. While you may experience these things intermittently and for brief interludes, you will never be able to own them. At the end of a relationship you can look back and see the times you were happy or feeling love. But if you are honest with yourself you will realize that most of your time in the relationship was spent in your mind. From the vantage point of your mind, you massaged and manipulated your partner to get what you felt you needed.

Asking "why" you behave in a certain way will only lead to more "whys." Answering "why" will have you chasing your tail. You will think you are getting somewhere but in the end you will have only exhausted yourself, or at the very least become quite dizzy. Even if you catch your tail, what have you caught? The tail is attached to the dog, which is attached to the tail...Neither chasing nor catching your problems will end problems. Nor will you find the ultimate solution. Finding out why you behave a certain way only encourages you to delve more deeply into your difficulties. Remember, your problems are not the problem. Your suffering will not end by changing your behavior. *Your behavior will change by ending your suffering.*

When something goes wrong it shakes us awake. As soon as we wake up to the fact that something is wrong we try to fix it. The waking-up part is good. The fixing part is misguided. It is misguided because one-and-a-half thoughts after we wake up our memory kicks in and we slip back into autothink. That's right we wake up, fluff our pillow a couple of times, roll over and fall back asleep. Warm and cozy, we dream a wonderful dream, that the two "railway lines" will one day meet not on the horizon, but at our very feet.

The sword and the leaf

Be careful. These dreams are not benign. They are nightmares. If we do not wake up now we will be shaken awake, by the last convulsion of a dying world, to find that our nightmares are real.

My father was a warrior by profession and by deed. He fought in World War II, Korea and fought twice in the jungles of Viet Nam. He was not a very religious man but he was especially spiritual. In this regard he aligned more with the code of Bushido, the code of honor developed among the samurai, the military warriors of Japan. During World War II while fighting in the Pacific theater my father came by a katana, a samurai sword. As a boy, I remember him showing me the sword and explaining the significance that it had for the soldier who owned it. He told me that these swords were passed down from father to son as a symbol of the moral principles that support the spiritual warrior in war and during peace. He showed me the handle and told me that under the sharkskin wrapping was written the family history. He showed me the blade that I was not allowed to touch, and explained that the Japanese sword makers were the best in the world when this sword was made, almost 250 years ago.

My father said that the blade was imbibed with spiritual strength that both fed and was nurtured by the owner of the sword. Legend taught the spiritual power of a katana could be demonstrated by placing the blade in the path of a leaf as it flowed downstream. If the leaf hit the sword and wrapped around the blade the sword was spiritually weak. If the leaf was cut in half by the katana the sword was strong in the spirit of Bushido. However, if the floating leaf approached the sword and then flowed effortlessly around the blade without touching it, this was the sword of supreme spiritual power. Twelve years after the atomic bomb was dropped on Hiroshima my family moved to Yokohama, Japan. We had many Japanese friends and learned to love and respect the people and culture of Japan. During the three years we lived with the Japanese my father tried to find the family who owned the katana. Neither my father nor our Japanese friends were successful. Years later, before my father died he passed the sword on to me.

There have been great injustices performed on every strata of human life. War has been ever present. Country against country, clan against clan but in the end it is now, as it has always been, one person against another. Warring between countries is an illusion. A country cannot go to war, only its people can. We continue to expend copious amounts of rhetoric aimed at abolishing war. Documents of peace are written, as if the paper has the power. We shake our head at the evening news and wonder why people can't just get along and then shake a fist at a slow-moving driver on our way home to subjugate our spouse and children. The world is a violent place primarily because we have lost awareness of our Self in the frantic milieu of other Self-searchers. The world is a violent place because we all too easily see others as the cause of our pain—pain generated by our own unobserved Self. My father, and every other man, woman and child who has ever been at war, had to confront this issue and come to some sort of conditional peace to make sense of their lives. Some have been more successful than others but almost all fail to resolve the issue of war on the personal level. The answer is in the blade and the leaf. We can vanquish our enemies or yield to their aggression. It really doesn't matter. Until we generate our own personal power of Self, anything more involved than drawing our next breath will generate only more violence.

But the tigers come at night

It's not that we are incapable. We have the spiritual technology. We have always had it. We have just put it off in favor of more immediate stuff. We have embraced the world of dreams. The destruction of the world, the warring of nations and conflict between individuals all flow from the same fountain of fantasy. While we dream and hope for the future the present slips by unnoticed.

Our interactions with our world, our country, our jobs and families are, first and foremost, relationships. They exist, not to make us happy, but to make us aware. Whether we like them or not is secondary. The value of interaction is to wake us up to the Self in others. That's right. Relationships exist for us to find our Self in others. That is what becoming aware of another means. If we think interaction with others is to make us happy then we are focused on "me," the perfect formula for failure.

Waking up can be painful. The longer we sleep the louder the alarm clock has to ring. The troubles around the world and between individuals are growing graver by the day. Our alarm clock has become a smoke detector. It is a warning that imminent danger is at hand. And what do we do? We get angry at the noise for disturbing our sleep.

In the play Les Miserables, Fantine sings a song written by Alain Boublil & Claude-Michel Schonberg, called, *I Dreamed a Dream.*

My favorite part of the song goes like this:

> *But the tigers come at night*
> *With their voices soft as thunder*
> *As they tear your hope apart*
> *And they turn your dream to shame.*

Fantine has lost the man of her dreams, and now she is in great pain. The tigers have torn her hope apart and turned her dream to shame. The tigers are her alarm clock. Rather than pulling the covers over her head, she should embrace them and understand her time for dreaming has passed. Sitting on the edge of her bed, she should stretch a giant stretch, rub the sleep from her eyes and greet the day, the radiant Self, shining through the curtains.

Freezing God into form

Everyone that I know is involved in a relationship with at least one other person. (Obviously, if they weren't, then I wouldn't know them.) Inter-personal relationships are the focus of our discussion in this chapter. To break free from the dream-web our minds have spun we must step beyond the mind into pure Self. Likewise, to understand relationships completely we have to step back and look at another kind of relationship, the one between a human and his God. We forsake individual struggle for universal harmony when we interact with the mundane as if with God. When the stone in the palm of your hand reflects back the symphony of the spheres, suffering will be beyond your grasp.

Many of us look to God for protection and nurturing. If our perception is more classical (that is cause and effect related) we tend to perceive God as having some kind of form, usually human. When we humanize God we can communicate and interact with Him/Her in a way that is familiar to us. We talk to God much in the same way we talk to each other. When we perceive that things are not going our way we ask God to intervene and make them right. It is our experience that some humans in our lives have protected us and nurtured us. For most of us those humans were our parents, grandparents, spouses and a few others. We know how it felt to be loved unconditionally. We also experienced conditional love and learned that even the humans who love us are capable of causing pain.

Those human qualities get transferred to God. Many of us feel that our God has created a kind of spiritual obstacle course with the hurdles being pain, suffering and fear. This is how we are supposed to learn right from wrong. In theory, if we do well we get rewarded. Wrong action brings us only more pain. But our world is teeming with examples to the opposite. How many people have we read about or know personally who don't do good things and yet thrive as a result? Our answer to them is that they will get theirs in the end. But this is not always true either. Karma, the belief that good actions beget good and bad begets bad, is born of this mystery. Karma is supported by Christ's teaching that "as you sow, so shall you reap." It can foster a sour grapes or a "holier than thou" attitude depending on the person and the circumstance. The Karmic orientation is a classical orientation that actions and things are separate from God and Self. It tells us that we can control our lives by our actions. And it teaches us that doing good will earn us entrance into Heaven. But there is something seriously wrong with this approach to salvation.

It is true that Christ said, "As you sow, so shall you reap." He also said, "You can not get into Heaven by good deeds alone." Somewhere along the line we made an inductive leap out of the proverbial frying pan into the spiritual fire. Spiritual growth appears to be mirroring western scientific advances. Quantum physics does not eliminate the remarkable contributions by Newton and other classical physicists. It includes and expands upon them. Both views are complementary. But when we shift our perception from a localized, thing-oriented Newtonian view to a non-localized, unbounded quantum mechanical view, we expand our world view beyond simple cause and effect.

To appreciate this shift in perception from a spiritual perspective we must lose the form of God. Or, more accurately, expand the form of God beyond infinity, beyond form. It is our "idea" of God that has frozen Him into form. Of course God is in form, I am not saying that He is not. But He is much more. He is It. It includes He. By definition, God is everywhere all the time. A form, even the form of God, is limited to the boundaries of that form. If God is everywhere all the time, then He must not only be His form but He must be beyond His form. If He were not, then He would be limited and He would not be God.

Here is the problem. When we confine God to form we can never realize the magnitude of our ultimate importance. In our minds, we will always remain separate from God and separate from His creation. But if God is everywhere all the time, then we must be God too. How can we possibly be outside God? On the deepest level, when we separate ourselves from God in this way, it creates a sense of isolation and fear. This perception of isolation is the birth of ego.

The greater our feeling of isolation the more effort we put into finding God. The more effort we expend in our search the harder it is to find God. Haridas Chaudhuri, educator and philosopher of Eastern thought, echoes the futility of searching for perfection when he warns us that "The greater the emphasis upon perfection, the further it recedes." As long as we hold the idea that God is only a form we can never be completely at peace, for God is both formless and all form.

We hold onto God as form because we fear losing what we have. At least the form of God is better than nothing. Or is it? To embrace the fullness of God we have to be like a monkey swinging from branch to branch. We have to let go of what we have to move on. The idea of letting go and flying through the air may initially be frightening. But it is only a perception. When we actually do let go of our idea of God as form, the freedom we experience is beyond word and expectation. We lose nothing. We gain Eternity.

The ultimate relationship

At first glance there are three basic kinds of relationships that humans enjoy. These are human-to-human, human-to-nature and human-to-God relationships. In all three the element that remains the same is the human. It is the human who defines the relationship. Even the human-to-God relationship is defined by the mind of man. A fourth relationship exists and steps beyond the limitations of mind.

The fourth relationship is the God-to-God relationship. As soon as you read "God-to-God" some of you may have experienced an unexpected reaction. It may have been subtle but you may have felt a little isolated or left out or even a little irritated or sad. After all, God-to-God has eliminated the human element, and I am a human. Therefore, I cannot be a part of the God-to-God relationship. Not so. In fact, it is your birthright as a human to live the God-to-God relationship. Actually, you are living it. The trick is to realize it.

If you think I've gone "round the bend" on this one then I'm in good company. This perception that man is God has reverberated down through the ages by seers in every tradition.

Christ said, "Where I am there shall also my servant be." And about this quote Meister Eckhart elucidated, "So thoroughly does the soul become the same being that God is, no less, and this is as true as God is God."

Walt Whitman wrote in *"A Song for Occupations"*

> *We consider bibles and religions divine—I do not say they are not divine,*
> *I say they have all grown out of you, and may grow out of you still,*
> *It is not they who give the life, it is you who give the life,*
> *Leaves are not more shed from the trees, or trees from the earth,*
> *Than they are shed out of you.*

John M Koller, author and professor of oriental philosophies, bluntly illustrates how man cannot possibly exist separate from his God. He states, "If whatever is is dependent upon another, then any kind of "straight line" causality is ruled out. There are no independent beings that are responsible for the existence of dependent beings. For example, the theistic notion that one absolutely independent being—God—created the rest of what exists, and that created universe depends for its existence upon God, makes no sense...whatever creates is also created, and the process of creating and being created go on simultaneously without beginning or end."

Through the discriminative eye of science Erwin Schrodinger discovered, "Subject and object are only one. The barrier between them cannot be said to have broken down as a result of recent experience in the physical sciences, for this barrier does not exist."

And finally, exposing the illusory relationship between man and God, these words still inspire a sense of space and undulating impermanence centuries after Shankara spoke them.

> *Though difference be none, I am of Thee,*
> *Not Thou, O Lord, of me;*
> *For of the sea is verily the Wave,*
> *Not of the Wave the Sea.*

Like the assimilation of Newtonian physics by quantum physics, the God-to-God relationship assimilates the other three human-oriented forms of interaction. You see, there is only one possible relationship to be had, and that is God-to-God. The other three are only illusions, divisions for the sake of convenience. A relationship becomes human when the human mind is in charge. It becomes Divine when the mind and the rest of the world are observed. What is doing the observing? Self. What is Self? It is unbounded Energy, Intelligence and Love. Self is God. Observing is innerthinking, God becoming aware of God. That is, God becoming aware that all things and nothing is It Self!

When you look at a flower, you are either relating human-to-nature or God-to-God. The only difference is whether you are awake at that moment. If your mind is autothinking, then you are interacting with the flower human-to-nature. However, if you are paying attention, then God perceives God through the medium of God. That's all there is to it.

Do you remember experience one in Chapter One when you first stopped your thinking? At first you saw it as a gap, a space between thoughts. Mental content was suspended and only awareness remained. Repeating the experience, the gap got bigger and you recognized that the space was not dead, but vibrantly alive. Then you were faced with a paradox. If you were not thinking and your mind was free of content, then how were you aware that there were no thoughts? You, Pure Awareness were observing you, Pure Existence. Self had become aware of Self. In this single innocent experience, God found God!

You became aware of Self when thoughts shut off. When they started up again you were able to continue observing. Before thoughts, Self was observing Self. After thoughts, Self was still observing Self, only now Self had taken the form of thoughts. Thoughts were formed out of Stillness, the silent Self. Thoughts are things. Other things, trees, stars and cars, are also Self that have taken form. When you observe any form with complete awareness you will find its shimmering essence to be nothing other than You, the Self. This is the God-to-God relationship. It does not matter whether you are observing another human, nature or your own personal form of God. When you are innerthinking you are God becoming aware of God.

Angels look at humans and just shake their heads. These "lower" beings with muddled, misdirected minds, and vulgar bodies filled with phlegm and gas, are the same beings who can transcend even the exalted celestial realms and know the Unknowable. The human is unique in this regard. She is capable of experiencing the deepest hell and the highest heaven all in a single lifetime. This gift of extremes opens her awareness to the fullest expression of creation. After all, what does an angel know of suffering? With feet in the mud and head in the heavens, the human awakens to the fullness of creation.

This enlightened soul moves amongst us lightening our load without being burdened herself. She is like the fairest thought drifting above the heaviness that is human. The enlightened soul is free from suffering but her expanded awareness has a price. After the suffering has slipped away there remains a kind of cosmic sadness. Her world is beyond all others and yet she is still touched by our suffering. All is perfection save for that chamber of her heart where she holds her love of humanity. Her relationship is with the whole, not the parts. She cannot be fully free while others suffer. For her the perfect relationship will not spread its wings and take flight until every cocoon has birthed its butterfly.

Our part in a relationship is this, to take responsibility for our own awareness. The rest will take care of itself. This is a leap of faith for most and reality for the rest. Our partner doesn't need to stop squeezing the toothpaste from the top of the tube. We need to be aware. That is it. That is how simple it is. The perfect relationship starts and ends with awareness of the Self. When Self-awareness dawns, the binding threads of our cocoon loosen and finally fall away, releasing a fully aware soul into the world.

MAIN POINTS FOR CHAPTER THIRTEEN

The Perfect Relationship

- No two people can ever have exactly the same point of view.

- "I" loves without reason and "me" looks for reasons to love.

- Love created by "me" is conditional love.

- Your Self will not allow conditional love to survive for long.

- Your suffering will not end by changing your behavior. Your behavior will change by ending your suffering.

- Relationships encourage us to find our Self in others.

- We forsake individual struggle for universal harmony when we interact with the mundane as if with God.

- If God is everywhere all the time, then we are God too.

- The perfect relationship starts and ends with awareness of the Self.

CHAPTER 14

How To Not-Know

"All knowledge is ignorance."

Nisargadatta

"Simplicity is the ultimate sophistication."

Leonardo da Vinci

We know we can but believe we can't

I hate to start a chapter with a disclaimer but that is exactly what I am going to do. If I did not, I'm afraid that analytical mind that needs to understand everything right now might end up with a debilitating migraine for its efforts. What is laid out in the paragraphs that follow has to be said. Otherwise, this book would be incomplete. If it makes sense to you go with it, if it does not...go with it anyway. Reading "How to Not-Know" will give you plenty of opportunities to practice presence. I also want to take this opportunity to underscore the fact that peace is not the result of knowledge. Let the words come and go without trying to hold on. The exploration of Not-Knowing is utterly fascinating and completely beyond the grasp of the mind. Look at it as one long koan, the ultimate cosmic joke, for it is cosmic humor at its best. So as my father used to say, "Stand down and take your packs off, troops, it's time to have some fun."

The vision we have of our potential, personal and collective, is colorless, faint and one dimensional. This is true even if you aspire to save the world. The senses feed the mind and the mind directs the senses and so through the unfolding of time our linear lives evolve to their ends. Compared to the vastness of creation we are less evident than a freckle on an electron's backside. We wear blinders and "walk the line" because we believe in our teachers as they believed in theirs. I once had a friend tell me that people don't really change. I asked her why she had taken my class. She said she wanted more peace in her life. "Why bother," I asked, "if people don't really change?" Humans are a conundrum, a kind of circular, unsolvable puzzle. We know we can, but we believe we can't.

145

We have living within us warring views, each compelling us in opposite directions. On one hand, we have an innate drive to expand, grow, evolve and eventually be complete. On the other, we see generations upon generations of failure evolve past the most elemental and destructive animal like-behavior. We don't "think" it can be done because it never has. A rasping sigh from somewhere within our deepest darkness pleads, "Is this all there is?"

Of course this is not all there is. This is only how it has been. We are wearing blinders. If you look only in front of you that is where you will go, and that is all you will know. Removing our blinders is simple but seldom easy. It takes commitment, courage and energy. Removing our blinders is at once natural and uncommon. It goes against our outer training but with our inner flow. Initially, opening to the fuller promise of fulfilling our potential can be confusing and even a little unsettling. But, with a little patience our blinders will fall at our feet and be forgotten. The brilliance of this world is without shadow.

Life as a line in the dirt

Many of us picture the course of our lives like a line drawn in the dirt. Where we first place the stick is our birth. The line drawn from there represents our life's experiences and the spot where we lift the stick from the dirt represents our death. Some say that is the end of it all, others say there is a soul that abides in Heaven for eternity and still others believe the soul returns to draw another line in the dirt. For our purposes here it does not matter which view or variation you may feel real. Our present focus is linear life lived between the placing and the removing of the stick. Linear living is limited living in the land of the living dead. (Say that 3 times fast!)

There is another model of life that is gaining greater popularity in these more fruitful days of quantum mechanics. I will call it the record model. Now there I've gone and dated myself. I'd better use the more contemporary CD model. By using the word "record" I will have my younger readers quizzically angling their heads like the R.C.A. Victor dog in front of a victrola.

The CD model goes like this. Instead of a straight line, our lives are like the concentric circles on a CD that thread together the songs of our life. The continuous line could represent a single life. Or if you believe in reincarnation each song on the CD could represent a separate life. Again, it really doesn't matter here because bending the life line has the same result for one life or for many. Instead of past and future lives you can substitute the memories and hopes of this life for each song and the model will still work. If you are halfway through the CD, you could be mid-life or in the middle of 10,000 lives, the point is, from the middle you can skip laterally and experience your future or your past. Let's say, due to some outside force like bumping up against the CD player, the laser needle jumps to another track. If the laser needle jumps one way you are in the past, the other opens you to your future.

The DVD model

Let's expand this model to include all life, all of creation. Let us also add video and call it the DVD model. Now, skipping tracks would be like jumping to other parts of the universe. It would be like a wormhole in our consciousness allowing us to peer into other worlds, thus making them part of our world.

Basically, what we are doing is stepping back from our line-in-sand lives and getting a bird's-eye view of life. The universe is not linear. And this brings up an interesting idea. We can enjoy the sights and sounds when we play the DVD because electromagnetic impulses are captured and stored there. When the laser needle passes over the stored impulses it sends the information to the player and we see the images just as they were recorded even years before.

These electromagnetic impulses represent thoughts and actions, places and events frozen in time. A single cluster of impulses could reflect the entire life of a single person caught on that part of the DVD. When the laser passes over the stored impulse it bursts to life on our television screen. After the laser leaves the impulse it returns to a frozen seed of sight and sound. In actuality, the laser acts more like an electromagnetic magnifying glass. It moves in close enough for us to see the form, the unique patterns of energy that we can recognize. Remember, everything in creation is energy frozen in form. A car, the stars and your best friend are just that, familiar patterns of frozen energy.

We began with a one-dimensional line in the sand representing our life. Even though the life line is one dimensional it is lived in the four dimensions of space-time. So what's the problem, you ask? The problem is space and time. We still believe that the human is obligated to live in space-time. After all, with the exception of the teachings of a few rare individuals in every generation, that's the way it's always been. We have in essence accepted the teachings of those who were bound by space and time and virtually ignored the paradigm presented by those who have slipped those binding chains. Of course I'm referring to the great human luminaries like Christ, Buddha and Shankara, Einstein, Socrates and Lao Tze. And to all of those lesser known shooting stars who, while humankind sleeps, silently light up midnight skies.

The DVD model provides some insight as to how we can expand our vision beyond the bounds of space-time. The key to unlocking the DVD model is not in the structure of the DVD but in the laser light that sweeps across it. The structure of the DVD contains frozen energy in the form of information. It virtually stays the same. But when the laser light falls on that packet of information, it briefly illuminates and liberates the information and then moves on. It is this movement of laser light that creates the sense of time. There is a beginning, middle and end to the DVD movie that is our life. The laser dutifully moves along its circular path awakening our phenomenal universe one thought at a time. If the laser skips you can see the end of the movie before you see the middle. But that is not desirable because it offends our sense of chronological order. Beginning, middle, end; that is the way it has to be. End of discussion. Beginning, middle and end, just like a line drawn in dirt.

I can already feel some of you protesting. Who would want to watch a movie with the end in the middle? That's just ridiculous. And I agree with you. Knowing the end before its time is very frustrating to me when I am locked in space-time. I have returned defective DVDs to the store and huffed, "This was a waste of my time."

I did not get what I wanted. It frustrated me just like my life does when I'm living in time and out of order. There is no sense of rhythm, no sense of control. Then I realize that it is the expectation of order that causes discomfort, not the actual disorder itself. One of the most beautiful and inspiring DVDs I have seen has no apparent order or obvious theme. Baraka is a series of impressions from all over the world. It presents people and places in no discernable order and no commentary. That's right, we are not told a thing. By the end of the experience a deeper, more compassionate connection was cultivated with my world on a level impossible to reach with a conventional beginning-middle-end DVD. I have watched Baraka many times with friends and their response is always the same. They express a sense of expansion and wonder that they can not describe in words. We have been taught that linear thinking, like linear living, is the eventual road to overcoming our problems and living in peace. Despite the description of a different, non-linear multi-dimensional thinking by our great philosophers and scientists, we refuse to let go of the idea that a beginning-middle-end approach to life is the only way to succeed and feel complete. It is in fact this dogged determination to break through all barriers and arrive at an end that has kept us savoring the infinite flavors of suffering offered us through space-time.

Do we have to throw out logic and analytical thinking? No, of course we don't. Obviously there is great power in thinking things through. We don't have to give it up. We just have to let go of the idea that it is the way. If you are not convinced just look at the great knowledge we have amassed with it. And then look at how close we may be to extinction because of it. Linear thinking is mind-made and out of control. The chisel is using the sculptor.

Let's get back to our DVD model and the problem with linear thinking. You could say that a DVD is nothing more than a straight line that has been bent. And you would be right. Even when the laser skips laterally to the future or past it is doing so linearly. So, what's all this hubbub about? If the laser needle skips laterally from past to future and back again it only changes the sequence in time. It does not eliminate time itself. In essence, the skipping laser needle breaks beginning-middle-end thinking and replaces it with a kind of "wait and see what happens" thinking. Waiting to see what happens is still time-dependant.

Upon inspection you will find that the laser needle, like its observable precursor the record needle, does not move. The DVD spins while the laser waits for the next packet of information to arrive. This is an important point. The laser is stationary and the information comes to it. Aren't we like the needle? We have a sense that we are moving through life. But are we? Do our bodies really carry our consciousness from place to place? That certainly isn't true when we imagine or dream or remember. Is it possible that ego's need to control creates the illusion that we move out into the world to survey and conquer? Is it possible that the world actually comes to us? The DVD model tells us that it is.

In our house we appear to move from room to room. We move from one person to another throughout the day, throughout the years. We move from childhood to adulthood and then old age. Through it all we are the focal point as the rest of our world materializes and then passes into memory. The next time you are driving down the highway, imagine that you and your car are stationary and the scenery is actually moving past you. This is a simple, delightful exercise that helps to shift our perspective from the active to the passive. We are like the laser light and the DVD is our world. As the world passes by we light it up with our consciousness. What our consciousness does not discover, for all intents and purposes does not exist.

Our consciousness is where we are. It is localized and waiting to see what will next appear. In this sense we have a one-directional view of the world. We are wearing blinders. The whole cosmos exists and we experience only our infinitesimal slice of it. Herein lies the problem. Both the Line in Dirt and the DVD models represent our consciousness, precisely limited in a linear model in space and time. Basically, what you see is what you get.

Is there another way of "seeing" that is complete, a way of perceiving that opens our consciousness to the fullness of creation? Many have said so. Christ was among them. He taught, "Recognize what is in your sight, and that which is hidden from you will become plain to you. For there is nothing hidden which will not become manifest." Christ is clearly pointing at an alternate awareness that will open the laser-like consciousness to what is hidden from it. But what is it? How does it work?

The holographic DVD model

A DVD is a flat disc. The pictures and sounds it produces are two dimensional. What if we could make a spherical DVD that would project three-dimensional pictures? We would have a hologram. A hologram is simply a three-dimensional picture created with a laser. The three dimensions of space; length, width and height plus time are what Einstein called space-time. Space-time is where we live. We navigate and manipulate things. Our minds think and feel in space-time. Our thoughts and feelings are rich and full and flow freely in the river of time. After all, that's life. What else could there be? Indeed, what else could there be?

Instead of a flat disc with data or information on the surface we would have a sphere stuffed full of information. The information would be holographic. That is, each piece of information would be connected to every other piece of information. Rather, each packet of information would be the same information in a different form. Or to be perfectly precise, all the information would be the same until our laser needle consciousness focused on it. Then it would take form or be expressed and interpreted in the way best suited for our needs.

Confused? Hang in there. This holographic view is actually easier to grasp than our traditional linear one once you understand how a hologram is made. In our world a piece of information would appear to take the separate forms of a chair, black jelly beans or a leaf. They appear unrelated to each other except in the most obvious and direct ways you may interact with them. When you sit in your favorite chair next to your prize schefflera and eat a hand full of black jelly beans you can see how these normally unrelated objects fit together. When you leave the room they lose the relationship they just shared. Their relationship is defined by you on a need by need basis. It is not so with a hologram.

The interesting thing about a hologram is that every apparent packet of information contains complete information about every other packet in the hologram. If you cut in half a traditional two dimensional picture of your pet schnauzer Ginger, you will find half of Ginger on one piece and the other half of her on the other piece. But if you cut a hologram of Ginger in half you end up with two complete holograms of Ginger, only smaller. (This process of procreation eliminates the expense of a stud service but also the "pick" of the litter.) The information in the two-dimensional picture is localized and subject to separation and fragmentation. It is impossible to destroy the integrity of the holographic picture no matter how many pieces you may cut it into. The same point can be made about our lives as pertains to consciousness. Two-dimensional consciousness bound in the chains of space-time continually experiences separation and fragmentation. Actually, that is a good working definition for this life. Holographic consciousness however, is forever whole. Holographic consciousness, now that's a mouthful. You may be asking yourself what hat I pulled that one out of. Let's find out.

One fish, two fish, red fish, blue fish

In 1982, physicist Alain Aspect discovered that subatomic particles like electrons communicate with each other over vast distances, even millions of light years. What is astonishing about this discovery is that the communication happens instantaneously even at opposite ends of the universe. Einstein showed us that faster-than-light communication is impossible. So how can this be? David Bohm suggested that these subatomic particles are not really separate entities but two expressions of a much subtler energy/intelligence system. He said that we only perceive them to be separate.

To illustrate he explained it in this way. You are in one room and a fish in an aquarium is in another room. You are not told how many fish are in the aquarium. Someone has set up two video cameras so that you can see the fish. One camera is in the front of the aquarium and the other is pointed at the side. When you look at the two monitors you initially think that there are two fish, not one. That is because you see one image of the fish from the front and the other from the side. But soon you notice that the two fish tend to move in some kind of synchrony. They float up and down together and when one turns to the side the other turns to face you. You might think that the fish were somehow communicating with each other. Bohm suggested that we were observing one electron from two different angles. In a linear universe this could not happen because of the restraints put on a single observer bound by space-time. That observer is limited by laser-like consciousness. If the universe were a hologram then this observation would be possible, and a great deal more.

At the risk of having Dr. Bohm turn over in his grave, I would like to take the liberty to expand his aquarium analogy to further a very important point. Let's add another camera, this one at the top of the aquarium. The third camera is sonar. When you see the sonic waves on your monitor you have no idea that it represents echoes bouncing back from the fish. You may think that the camera is broken or picking up some kind of electromagnetic static. The different camera angle and the sound waves have you puzzled. To you, they do not represent a fish at all. Now add infrared and x-ray cameras at oblique angles and you throw up your hands in complete frustration. A snickering scientist, drinking coffee in a stained lab coat, comes in to tell you that there is only one fish and that all the cameras are giving you the same information from different perspectives through different mediums.

"Oh," you say. And a second scientist quickly enters the room and tries to pry your fingers from around the first scientist's neck.

All of the data you received were about one fish. The information came to you in many different ways but still it was only a single fish. Your linear consciousness broke the data into separate packets. When the scientist explained how things worked, all the pieces of the puzzle fell into place. In our day-today lives objects and people and ideas and time and space all feel separate, like interacting electrons and trained fish. But they are not. Your life is a hologram. In you is contained all of the phenomenal worlds of creation. And here is how.

When the DVD spins it presents the information to be read to the laser. We have said that the laser represents our individual consciousness. We also pointed out that it feels like we are moving through life. This feeling of movement in time is created because we have a laser-like consciousness. It is acutely focused on what is directly in front of it. The sweeping of the information through our consciousness gives the illusion of time. But in actuality, time and space do not exist.

The dark room

Let's put you into another room only this one is completely dark. But you have a flashlight and you turn it on. The first thing you see is a blue Chinese vase. As you sweep the light around the room you illuminate a book, a picture and then a stale peanut butter and jelly sandwich lying stiffly next to a TV remote. Let's say the whole process took a minute. Then you shine the light on...me! After you catch your breath, I ask you to tell me what you did and how much time it took you to do it. You tell me that first you saw the vase, then the book, the picture and finally the sandwich next to the remote. Your consciousness followed the light around the room for one minute. When the light shone on the sandwich you were not thinking about the book. Was the book still there on the shelf? How do you know? For all intents and purposes, when your consciousness left the book it no longer existed. (I'll bet you didn't think the "when a tree falls in the woods" enigma would raise its ugly head again, did you?) Here's the deal. Linear consciousness gives up one thing for another. Holographic consciousness experiences the essence of everything, all at once. This is pure awareness. In this analogy, holographic consciousness would be like flipping on the light switch flooding the room with light. Pure awareness is the light. The vase, book, picture and PB&J sandwich appear in the same place (the room) at the same time. And not just those objects. Although you may focus on a single object, effectively every object in the room could be seen, or sensed, all at once. You do not need to sweep your laser-consciousness flashlight from object to object. You actually experience a focused consciousness within a generalized awareness. In effect, you are everywhere at once. By turning on the light you turned off space and time.

Nothing is not empty

Let's exchange our room for the entire cosmos. All the things of creation, star dust and anti-matter and ladybugs and sweet dreams, are contained within this cosmic egg, this holographic DVD. It is surrounded by Nothing. Nothing is not empty. Nothing has all the building blocks to fill our cosmic egg with an infinite multiplicity of things but they have not yet taken form. Bohm calls Nothing "implicate order." The first two verses of Genesis reflect, "In the beginning...the world was without form, and void; and darkness was upon the face of the deep." The echo of Nothing is also heard in the first line of the Taittiriya Upanishad, "In the beginning the world was not."

Then Nothing became something. Genesis observes, "And the Spirit of God moved upon the waters. And God said, let there be light; and there was light." Taittiriya Upanishad further unfolds, "From non-existence came Existence. From itself Existence created the Self. Thus it is called the Self-Made." The Self, your Self came from Nothing. Self is the same as Nothing and a little different, but more on this in a moment.

Does something come from Nothing when you create something like a painting or a play house in the backyard for your kids? Yes and no. No, because the things you build come from other things. In order to create you collect your materials and your thoughts and prest-o chang-o, an ash tray from a lump of clay. But where did those materials and thoughts come from? They came from Nothing, of course. You already know that from the "Stopping Your Thinking" experience. Or as Taittiriya explains, "Truly, what the Self-Made is, is the Essence of existence."

Why would Nothing want to *appear* as something, as the phenomenal world? Because It could. If Nothing could appear as something but did not do so then it would not be living up to Its potential. (Nothing brings a whole new meaning to the slogan, "Be all that you can be.") Nothing would be incomplete. It would be partially empty and we already know that Nothing is not empty. On the other hand, if it really became something it would no longer be Nothing. What a quandary for Nothing. How could It be something and still be empty? Or, how could it not be something and not be empty? For the answer read my next book...O.K., O.K. So how did Nothing avoid the oblivion of emptiness and still not become something? It *appeared* to be something it wasn't. This is how the master Magician has pulled the wool over our eyes for all these many millennia. Few have seen through the illusion. For the rest of us this simple trick has withstood the test of time. (No pun intended.)

So what we have is the essence of Nothing appearing as everything. What that means is that Nothing is not separate from what It creates. It is Its creation. Everything, including you, is Nothing. Other names for you are Self-Made, or just plain

Self. If you are Self then you are the "Essence of existence." You are in everything. And why does any of this really matter? Because when you "know thy Self " you can know anything, and *then you will know Nothing*. (Did the light in your dark room just go on?) When you know thy Self, fear of the unknown is impossible. Fear of any origin is impossible. Or as Taittiriya Upanishad puts it, "Truly, it is this Essence that bestows Peace."

Creation did not happen

The final realization is that creation never happened. "Well," you say, "That is about the most ridiculous thing I have ever heard." If you are English you might just say, "Preposterous!" And It truly is inconceivable. But let's take a run at it anyway for those who can't quite accept that the intellect has limitations. What have we got to lose except possibly a few misconceptions and the anxiety that accompanies them?

I have said that our universe (holographic DVD) is surrounded by Nothing. It is also infused with and supported by unbounded Nothing at the same time. Or to be exact, all at the same "no-time." Thoughts are obligated to express motion. Therefore we think of creation as an event that happened, and continues even now. In actuality, creation is not happening, nor did it ever happen. It just is. Creation does not come and go. That is the illusion created by the Master of misdirection. Our limited laser-like consciousness gets focused on only one piece of the universe creating the *illusion* of time. Creation did not come out of Nothing. It is Nothing! It always has been just what it is, a seeming wave of Self on the ocean of Non-Self. But the wave is not moving! If it were it would be expressing time. Just like the form of the wave, motion is also illusion. The motion of a car driving past is actually an infinite number of cars that exist at different stages of completion just like a movie is individual still pictures representing different stages of the story. Each picture is complete within itself and yet part of the story. Each story is complete and yet part of a greater story. The final story is that there is no story without the sweep of our limited, laser-like consciousness to create one. It appears that the car is moving when in reality it is our linear consciousness moving quickly from one "picture" of the car to the next. The little illusion is that the car is moving. The ultimate illusion is that our consciousness is moving. When, in actuality, nothing moves, when our limited individual consciousness expands fully, like turning on the light in a dark room, it comes to know everything all at once, without movement. The rift created by time and space is healed. The broken pieces of the holographic mirror are found to have always been whole. *If Nothing has never been created and will never be destroyed, and Nothing is absolutely still, then how can there be movement?*

When the "Spirit of God" moved upon the waters there was actually no movement at all. There was only the appearance of movement. Remember, the Spirit of God is omnipresent and therefore has to be unmoving. Where could God go that God wasn't already there? The Bible, as with all holy texts, is the written word aimed at those who do not know God completely. Those of us who don't know God, by definition, are unaware of that unborn, undying, unmoving Presence. The words of the Bible, Koran and Bhagavad-Gita are as planks of a bridge. The bridge is meant to take you over "troubled waters" to God. But word bridges can only take common consciousness so far. The mind is left on the other side of the gap from whence thoughts come. The last plank of the bridge is intuition from which we must ultimately leap naked into Nothing.

If your mind is balking at this whole idea of the timeless, unmoving illusion of creation then your mind is doing what it must do. If you step outside your mind's control you will "know" Nothing to be true. Initially you may appreciate only a glint of knowing before swarms of killer thoughts swoop in to confound your cognition. But it is always there, and it will grow. The best advice I can offer at this point is to read and retire within your Self. Do the experiences in this book and be with your Self. Logic and analysis and intuition are born of Self. And like iron filings at a magnet, they will align with the experience until even experience falls away and Nothing is left.

Knowledge, knowing and not-knowing

Knowledge is the result of gathering data to add to our understanding. The two legs of knowledge are understanding and experience. Both legs are necessary if one wants to move forward. In walking, one leg supports the body while the other swings forward. Then that leg becomes the support so the other leg can swings forward. When understanding and experience are coordinated in balance and time, we progress.

You can also look at gaining knowledge like building a strong brick wall. The bricks are the understanding and the mortar is experience. If you build your wall with just bricks your wall will be well defined but lack strength. It will not survive the strong winds of scrutiny. If, on the other hand, you build your wall only of mortar it will be very strong but amorphous. It will lack organization. But when you alternately lay bricks and mortar you end up with a well defined structure that is also very strong.

Knowledge is relative and changes with time and circumstances. If we feel that we know something because we are able to label it or understand how it works we are fooling ourselves. Knowledge is always and only partial. Not until you think that you know something are you displaying ignorance of the whole. And that is when your troubles arrive with their suitcases stuffed full of facts, opinions and plans. For as we have learned, no thing really exists. To mistake a thing for being anything other than Nothing is to own only a single piece but believe that it is the entire puzzle. Nisargadatta, a wonderfully subtle saint from the 20th century said, "All knowledge is ignorance." He knew that the pursuit of peace through knowledge gathering could only end in more suffering.

Have you ever had a child with a budding intellect ask you "why"? No matter what you answer they simply ask again, "why?" It doesn't take too many whys before you run out of answers. You might then think that a scientist or poet might be able to answer all the whys. But sorry to say, they don't have all the answers either. Contrary to what we may feel we will never have all the answers to all the whys. It just ain't-a-gonna-happen. There seems to be a direct correlation between how much data we collect and how dangerous we become. We have never had more knowledge nor been greater danger of self-annihilation. Knowledge is fodder for the ego's plan to rule its world.

For years I have heard people say, "The more you know, the more you know you don't know." They are expressing the subtle frustration that we all feel when we try to control our world by becoming more knowledgeable but fail at finding peace. There is knowing and there is Knowing. Let's capitalize the last word in the foregoing saying and see what happens. "The more you know, the more you know you don't Know." Now, let's find out what we've done.

Intellect has the ability to learn by reason, the capacity for understanding. Therefore intellect is bound by space-time. Knowing (with a capital "K") is the cognition of the Devine Condition, oneness in the midst of diversity. This Knowing happens when you look deeply into a sky full of stars and feel mystery and awe and Know that you can never understand. But that's just fine because at that moment you don't need to understand. Grappling with the intellect in an effort to explain your feelings will only ruin the moment. And you will still not understand.

The self cannot exist without the fish

The transition from knowing to Knowing is innerthinking. It is the first fluttering of the gossamer wings of Self in mind. First experienced as a subtle nudging from somewhere beyond our common consciousness, Knowing tenderly nurtures, guides and protects us. This is what we call intuition. Intuition is the tender expression of the Self reflected in the mind. Intuition is Knowing without and before analysis and logic. It enriches and supports both. Intuition is Knowing that Nothing has everything under control.

This is the state where you know you Know, but you don't know how you Know. The Self is the "Spirit of God" that looked upon the waters. In fact, Self does not exist until it sees something other than itself. The Self is defined by what it sees. No Self, no seeing and nothing to be seen. The fishes of the waters were Bohm's fish in the aquarium seen from infinite perspectives. The Self can not exist without the fish. That is why Self is both unbounded and limited.

Knowing needs no proof for it is a reflection of what "is" and that is beyond the capabilities of intellect. People who are sure of their knowledge immediately fix their position and limit their options. They have the cart before the horse. By becoming aware of the reflection of Nothing in the mind we invite the organizing power of the universe to take the reins. Then our limited knowledge becomes infused with absolute organizing power and infinite possibilities. And that is a very good thing. Limited knowledge is still necessary for navigating the day-to-day world but the source of suffering has been plucked out like the proverbial splinter from our eye.

In pre-dawn darkness a dewdrop hangs heavy on a leaf. As the first rays of dawn penetrate it, a pure light appears to radiate from within the drop. Looking closely you will see a clear but distorted reflection of the dewdrop's world floating within that glistening bead. It is a hologram, a story of the world that surrounds it, which cannot be fragmented. Before dawn that story lies silently frozen in darkness. When Self awareness dawns in the mind it is like the illumination of the dew. It Knows that the world is but a modest reflection of itself. If the mind does not reflect awareness of Self it mistakes the reflection for the reality.

Knowledge cannot beget Knowing. But Knowing is the source of all knowledge. Socrates knew the power of Knowing. When he invited us to "Know thy Self," he knew that understanding the Self is impossible. Those of us who have tried to know the self through understanding and experiences have created more confusion and frustration than we have eliminated. Knowing the Self has traditionally been the practice of knowing "me." If we were to try hard enough to gather enough knowledge about the Self to understand it, we would reach a point of complete frustration (remember Arjuna). Only when one surrenders can Knowing break like the dawn in our consciousness. When we give up the effort to know our Self and simply be our Self, a deliciously deep peace washes away the years of struggle. It is the first and universal expression of Nothing. But Knowing is not the end of the story. When the Self becomes aware of itself, that is Knowing. When the Self drops away and there is only pure awareness, that is Not-Knowing.

The knower comes and goes with the known

Self only exists when there is something to witness. It's a game Nothing plays with Itself. The silent ocean of Nothing appears to make a wave. Since everything is contained in Nothing and Nothing is aware, It is aware of the wave. When Nothing becomes aware of the wave we now have two things, awareness and a wave. The awareness of the wave is the individual expression of Nothing called the Self. Self depends on the wave. When the wave merges back into the ocean of Nothing the witness of the wave, the Self, loses its individual reason for being and dissolves back into pure awareness. So with the birth of the wave individual Self-awareness is also born. Wave is born, Self is born. Wave returns to ocean of pure awareness and Self dissolves with it. The Knower comes and goes with the known.

But don't be fooled. Nothing is aware. The Self is made of Nothing and is aware. The wave is made of Nothing and is also aware. Pure awareness is awareness of Nothing. Self-awareness is when the Self becomes aware of its own existence and says, "I Am." When it becomes aware of the wave it says, "I Am aware of the wave." When Self loses awareness of itself all it will have left is awareness of the wave. That is common consciousness. When Self maintains awareness of its own existence, that is Knowing. When the wave merges back into Nothing so does the Self, and that is Not-Knowing. It is clear that Sergeant Schultz on the "60"s sitcom "Hogan's Heroes" understood this very profound secret of universal peace and the power of Not-Knowing. In almost every episode the obviously enlightened prison guard would repeat his mantra of ultimate Not-Knowing, "I know nuh-tink (nothing), I know nuh-tink." What an inspiration to us all.

This whole exercise of making a wave and a Self to observe it is a game. The creation of Self is just an illusion along with the rest of creation. Remember, the wave is Nothing and Nothing just is. When Self remembers itself it remembers that it is Nothing. That is a very important realization. The next step in the game is that the Self realizes that the wave is also Nothing. The wave is not "over there" to be observed by the Self. The wave is Nothing which is also Self and so we have Self observing Self. Or more specifically, human Self observing object Self. At this point there is no separation between object and observer. The final cognition is yet to be made. It is realized when Self sees that not only is itself and the object Nothing but the space between them and beyond them is also Nothing. Nothing is everything! The ultimate cognition is that they, the Self and wave, never left the ocean of Nothing. It was only an illusion, a game Nothing amuses itself by creating illusions. It is like thinking, thought without movement. Why does Nothing amuse itself in this way? It does so because it can. If it did not then it would not be Nothing.

Hold onto your hats—A quick recap (Pun intended.)

Traditional knowledge is common consciousness caught in the web of space-time. This knowledge is created by the mind and changes with the event. This is our mind-created world of past and future, pain and fear. When we Know, we bring awareness into common consciousness. We now observe the world of space, time and suffering from the detached and balanced vantage point of Self. Self adds the element of non-change to our life. This is the delicate blossoming of innerthinking, when common consciousness becomes aware of itself. This is the witness that observes, "I Am,"

Once common consciousness becomes aware of itself perception of life begins to change. As Knowing, Self awareness becomes more refined. The reflection of peace and joy are recognized and reflected more and more completely. Finally the seat of the Self is cognized. When this happens the subtle arms of Self unfold to embrace...Nothing.

Common consciousness knows nothing of Self. It is the dew in darkness. Self Knows that Nothing is in all things. It is the dawn breaking in the dew. Not-Knowing Knows Nothing. It Knows that even the Self is Nothing. The Self only Knows Nothing in other things. For Self to Know Nothing completely it must become Nothing. When Self no longer is, Nothing is. Not-Knowing, like Nothing just is. Not-Knowing is as if the light in the dew drop suddenly become aware that it is all light, everywhere and that all things are made of that light. It is like flipping on the light switch in our dark room and all things are Known instantly without space and time.

Not-Knowing is expanding the breadth and depth of the laser light needle to include the whole holographic DVD. Instead of packets of information being brought into our narrow field of consciousness, our consciousness is expanded to cognize all fields at once. The illusion of space and time and things is laid bare. The advantage of the Not-Knower is that of no movement and of no other. No movement means It is timeless and no other means It is One. Not-Knowing has nowhere to go and no desire to be elsewhere. It is free to be. These powerful words from Nisargadatta demonstrate that he had cognized this subtle division between Knowing and Not-Knowing: "The knower comes and goes with the known. Knowing is movement. That which does not know is free."

Experience Eight
(How to not-know)

Just kidding! Although Not-Knowing can be done by looking at a blank page I have something more tangible for you to start with. Do this experience with *no expectations*. Don't look for anything in particular. Just pay attention as the experience unfolds. Have fun with it.

Experience Eight
(How to not-know)
(Please adapt this exercise to the geographical area of
the earth in which you presently find yourself.)

Sitting in your chair "feel your body" as you did in Experience Six in Chapter Thirteen. You can start by closing your eyes and bringing your awareness to subsequent areas of the body or just hold awareness on the whole body. Wait 5 or 10 minutes or until a lively awareness can be felt in your body. Keeping your eyes closed, become aware of the room and the position your body occupies in the room. Now feel your awareness lifting upwards out of your body. Look back and see that your body is still sitting in the chair in the room. Let your awareness float higher, through the building and above the roof top. Allow your awareness to continue to float upward, increasing speed as it goes. Watch as houses and countryside yield to an ever-widening view of cities and lakes and forests. Soon you can see your whole state, the surrounding states and then the whole of North and South America bounded by beautiful blue seas.

Still accelerating backwards, watch the continents slip silently by as the earth slowly and powerfully rotates on its axis. As you continue, the earth shrinks to accelerate into space. The cool blackness embraces you and stars appear in that blackness as thousands of pinpoints of pure, clear light. Now our tranquil moon slips quickly, silently past you and becomes a pinpoint itself against the earth. Soon the earth too is lost in the swarm of stars. Although you continue to accelerate it feels like you are floating because of the vastness of space. Next you pass through the enormous presence of the sun. It too falls quickly away to merge with the other stars.

As you continue accelerating backwards the trillions of stars begin to form into our galaxy. As our galaxy shrinks other galaxies appear as pinpoints of light around it. Then our own galaxy becomes a point of 168 Beyond Happiness light lost amongst the trillions of other galaxies. Still accelerating backwards the galaxies combine to form of a great oval. This Cosmic Egg of starlight is the sum total of all of creation. It continues to grow smaller and smaller until it too is a prick of light in the vast velvet blackness. Finally, with a wink it disappears and your awareness is left with...Nothing.

Remain aware of Nothing as long as you like. Actually you have no control over how long you are aware of Nothing. Not-Knowing will automatically return to Self-awareness. When that happens, let your awareness return to the room in which you are sitting, feeling the body. Become aware of the vibrating Nothing in your body for a few moments. Then in a single heartbeat, allow the room and your body to dissolve back into Nothing.

When your awareness becomes filled with other thoughts you can bring it back to the room and feeling the body and then back to Nothing. Do this effortlessly while the mind is fresh. As soon as any effort is felt stop and rest. You've done beautifully. Pat yourself on the back and go about your life in normal fashion. While the immediate value of this experience is quite profound the deeper values will surface over time and without looking for them.

MAIN POINTS FOR CHAPTER FOURTEEN

How To Not-Know

- What our consciousness does not discover does not exist.

- Nothing is not empty.

- It is impossible for moving thought to understand a motionless universe.

- All knowledge is ignorance.

- When Self becomes aware of itself, that is Knowing.

- Self only exists when there is something to be aware of. The Knower (Self) comes and goes with the known.

- For Self to Know Nothing completely I must become Nothing.

- When Self merges completely with Nothing it Knows all of creation as the illusion spun by Nothing.

- Not-Knowing occurs when Self observes its own essence, pure awareness, as the essence of all.

Free will and determinism

The discussion of free will vs. determinism has probably been raging since the first caveman took a wife and then stayed out late watching the game with his caveman buddies. The problem with the controversy between free will and determinism is that we have tried to explain it from the perspective of common consciousness. Common consciousness, as you will remember, is awareness filtered through ego. It divides the world into things. It sees differences and judges them to be either helpful or hurtful.

The free will/determinism argument will never be set to rest through the eyes of common consciousness. It is not until awareness of the Self dawns that the dispute fizzles out. Knowing the Self means knowing non-change and free will and determinism rely on change for their existence. Through the eyes of the Self they are infertile seeds unable to sprout new controversy. In fact, Self-awareness dissolves all controversy for all time. Here's how it happens.

The problem of free will

When you drink orange juice out of the carton or comb your hair or work a cross-word puzzle who is performing the action? You say "I drink," "I comb," and "I write." But do you believe that you are really performing the action? If you do you are experiencing ego manipulated common consciousness. If you are performing the same action but you know that it is happening beyond your individual will then you are Self-aware. Everything is exactly the same except for who takes authorship for the action.

That is the only difference between someone who is "enlightened" and someone who is not. There are no celestial bells ringing or angels singing your praise. They don't need a reason to celebrate, they do it anyway. Angels are like that. What is known as enlightenment is simply the shift in perception from me to not-me.

If you have the idea that there is something that you can do to initiate this perceptual shift, forget about it. That very impulse is ego orientated and dooms the doer to perpetual doing. You either have it or you don't. But don't throw in the towel just yet. Any confusion or disbelief is just ego's way of buying time until it can persuade you that you (ego) are still in control of your world. By the time you finish this chapter you may see things differently.

One way you can know if you are experiencing common consciousness right now is if you balked at the idea that you could do nothing to bring about the state of Self-awareness. However, when you fully accept that there is nothing you can do, Self-awareness will dawn. You will recognize it by the peace and lightness that ensue.

Let's start by asking, "Are you certain that you really do have free will?" If so, demonstrate it to me by lifting your arm right now. Did your arm rise as you had dictated? It did? Well there you have it, a perfect example of the illusion of free will. I'm playing with you of course but the point is valid. If you believe your arm moved by your own resolve then you have been duped by your very own ego. Let's examine more closely this process of apparent free will.

Who had the thought that made your arm move? Again you say, "I did, I generated the thought. Then the thought did what thoughts do and then my arm moved." Now tell me where that thought came from? Did you consciously make it up? Or at my suggestion did you think, "He wants me to raise my arm. I can do that." Then you looked over at your arm and it lifted into the air. When thinking about it afterward you said, "I moved my arm." *Thinking about moving your arm and then watching it move does not necessarily mean that you were the one who moved it.* It could mean that this was going to happen anyway and you were simply there to observe it.

First of all, it was my suggestion that gave you the thought to move your arm. You could say that it was my thought that raised your arm into the air. Then it is only natural to ask how that thought came to me. There is a sort of chain reaction going on that is beyond our control. These reactions are going on all over creation and we are not aware of them. But all action is related by association with the source of those actions. And we know that all the inter-connectedness of all things comes from Nothing. We are only aware of those actions and reactions taking place in our little corner of the universe. Isn't that true? Our limited view isolates us and gives us a proprietary perspective. We don't see the whole picture. From our limited viewpoint we miss the primal causes of our present condition and their far-reaching results. This leads us to believe that we are in control, at least in our little corner of creation. In other words, we take credit for what comes from the Source.

"But" you say, "if I don't want to move my arm then it won't move." The same logic applies in this case, only in the negative. What universal chain of events preceded your decision? Where did you get the thought to "not move" your arm?

Have you noticed that every thought or action seems to be a response to a previous thought or action? You scratch your nose in response to an itch. You breathe out because you last breathed in. You get angry, sad, or fall in love because of how your genetic makeup had been imprinted by your environment.

If you really do have free will then it is only fair to ask how strong and far-reaching it is. If you have free will do you have it all the time? What if your arm had fallen asleep while you were reading and when you willed it to move it just lay there like a side of beef? Wouldn't you have been surprised? Or what if you willed it not to move and found that it reflexively swatted at a mosquito that had landed on your nose? Just because the light turns on almost every time you flip the switch does not mean that you are in control of the process. You can will your finger to flip the switch but your finger may miss the mark or you may get distracted by the UPS lady and forget to turn the light on at all. About all you can really say is that you have the initial thought to perform the action. Whether or not the action is completed the way you planned is totally beyond your influence.

Who thought the thought?

At this point, actual free will has been reduced to the single, initial thought that may set events in motion but has no control over their results. If this tenuous link to free will were cut then one would lose all hope of possessing individual free will. And losing hope, as we already know, is a good thing.

Remember when you observed the gap between thoughts and then continued to observe while thought started up again? You didn't produce those thoughts, did you? Thoughts spontaneously appear and disappear on your screen of consciousness by no volition of your own. They appear out of nowhere, or should I say Nothing. Then, after they are there for a split second, "me" rushes in and takes credit for producing that thought. In every instance, the thought was there before "me" noticed it and decided to take authorship.

Still not convinced? Let's take a look at what you are made of, what makes up "me." Ramesh Balsekar was a frequent visitor to the home of Nisargadatta and has authored numerous books about the relationship between "me" and "I" as we have defined them in this book. In his book *Peace and Harmony in Daily Living* he tells us that "me" is like a computer. A computer receives input which then produces an output according to its software. The computer controls neither input nor output. It just does what its software allows it to do. Balsekar says that humans are just like computers except we have an ego that takes credit for the input and the output. That is the only difference.

He supports his claims with the following logic. We are the result of the union of egg and sperm neither of which we have control over. We are expelled from the womb complete with genetic hardwiring which we did not choose, into an environment that we have no control over. The environment inputs impressions into the body/mind computer that is "me." There reactions automatically take place that create thoughts, desires, hopes and dreams. Then the output actions spill into the environment which in turn reacts and starts the whole process over again. At any given moment you are simply reacting to your world as a bundle of unique genes conditioned by the environment. You have no choice. You have to think and react just as you do. How could you act any differently?

For instance, if you decided to become more spiritual, that precise act of will would be the direct result of your genetic makeup and conditioning by your environment. If you decided to chuck it all and move to a desert island, that too would be the direct result of your genetic makeup and conditioning. If you decided to panhandle dollar bills for hamburgers that you would gladly repay on Tuesday; that too is the direct result of your genetic makeup and conditioning by your environment. Are you beginning to see that you may not have as much control as you originally thought? How could you choose to act outside the influence of your genes and the impressions your surroundings have imprinted on you? Whatever thought you have or action you perform is the direct result of the unique blending of both genetic hardwiring and environmental software. This blend of the two is what you have come to know as "me."

If we are to pursue this line of reasoning further we have to ask where our genes and environment come from. What is their primal cause? Obviously they came from the source of all things: Nothing. Nothing is simultaneously beyond and within all of creation including our genes and environment. That we can only intuit. We have seen that the most ancient spiritual texts and the most modern theories of science seem to point to an apparent universe that comes from the void of Nothing. Creation is the expression of the infinite intelligence of that Source. Every thought, emotion, sub-atomic particle or corporeal object is bathed in that infinite intelligence. There are no mistakes in nature, and as it turns out there are none in the world of humans either. Mistakes and problems are only perceived to be so. Even our perceptions of imperfection are in reality expressions of perfection. All actions, no matter what where or when, can never be outside the influence of that infinite Intelligence.

Karl Renz, in his book *The Myth of Enlightenment*, puts it this way, "Simply see that any contribution you made always happened on its own. It operated on its own and didn't need your decision. You fear that, without your decision, nothing would happen, but that's just an idea." He goes on to say, "Nothing depends on you...Every idea is spontaneous, every apparent decision comes out of nothing, out of the blue, from the great beyond. It has no direction. In fact, nothing has a direction."

The problem, if we can call it that, lies in thinking that we can create. Take for example the folding of a piece of paper into an airplane and sailing it across the room. In the deepest sense, where did the water and earth come from to make the tree that became the paper? Why did the plane land where it did and not somewhere else? What inspired the synaptic activity that created the thought to fold that paper? It all came from Nothing. It is only our very, very narrow vision of creation that convinces otherwise.

It is what it is

Theory is all fine and dandy, but how does this perceptual shift from being the creator to just going along for the ride play itself out in our day-to-day lives? Let me give you an example. Now don't look for any fireworks. There is nothing flashy about this experience, and because it is not flashy, many of us don't get it.

I was having lunch with a colleague and the conversation got around to perceived troubles in the office. He began describing the problem people and the negative circumstances they created. He was frustrated that he could not perform his job as he felt it should be carried out. I saw his point and agreed with him, citing my own grievances and how I also felt restricted. Then, because of decades of "spiritual" training I became aware of a wee small voice saying, "You shouldn't be complaining, Frank." Then I habitually started to temper my comments and guard my thoughts. I began acting the way I felt a pure soul without negative baggage would act. I also felt some amount of guilt at being so negative in the first place. I actually felt worse "being good" than I did when I was naturally negative. One thing I didn't feel was peace. That is a dead giveaway that all is not right with your world.

Then there was another shift. I got tired of trying to be an ideal, to be someone I wasn't. It was as though my mind took a big sigh and surrendered to what was. Through no volition of my own I simply realized that everything that was taking place was perfect just as it was. The negative emotions, the controlling behavior, and this final realization of perfection were all on equal footing. I was negative because that's the way "me" was created. I was good for the same reason. Sure, what was happening was the result of genes and training but it was more than that. My internal dialogue, our outward discussion about work, the stain on the waiter's apron and every word uttered and added to make up the constant din of our fellow diners was perfect. I had nothing to do with it. It was then that I noticed the peace. It came with a sense of awe at the utter mundaneness of it all.

The conversation continued and at times I found myself saying things that previously I would have considered negative. Sometimes I tried to fix those things and sometimes I just observed as the negative thoughts and words came and went. In every case they were in perfect synchrony with every other created thing, known and unknown. They were not, after all, my doing. It was as if I had washed my hands of this whole "life" thing and just settled into my Self and watched as my world unfolded one mundane moment after the next. They belonged to the Source and I was merely a spectator to the wonder of it all. I was not a spectator as an outsider would be. On the contrary, I was both beyond and intimately a part of all that I observed. It seemed oddly natural to know that nothing was being created other than the appearance of creation as it unfolded before me and my friend across the table.

As the conversation continued I doubt that he noted my awakening unless it registered on some subtle level where we all intuit the rightness of the world. At one point he was visibly concerned about how things were going to work within the company. I don't remember exactly what circumstances triggered his concern but I saw no problems. When he paused he looked at me for validation. My response was simple. I said, "It is what it is." And then we went on with our discussion as before. It was more of the same except, of course, I remained at peace. Some days later during a particularly discordant meeting I herd him say to another harried member of the team, "It is what it is." He smiled a gentle smile as if he had just recognized the mundaneness of his world.

To ask why things are the way they are reflects a desire to see beyond your slice of life, and know the primal mind and ultimate makeup of the universe. Somehow we feel that if we can understand the cosmic mind we will then understand our own. From there it should be a short leap to fixing the wrongs of our life and then we can live in peace and harmony. While a noble undertaking it is completely fruitless and still adds up to nothing more than ego's influence born of the need to collect enough pieces to make one whole. But you don't need to do that. The phrase "If it ain't broke don't fix it" comes to mind. If we feel incomplete we try and fix the perceived problem. The cosmic joke is on us, the thinking species. It is only the thought that we are not whole that makes us feel that we are not. When we let go of that thought we immediately realize that everything is just as it should be. You are already whole, not because I say so but because that is the fact. How could any product of Wholeness not be whole? Which is more likely, you are the incomplete product of the complete Creator or you just haven't realized your connection to that unbounded fullness? There is no why or how to be answered. Everything in this wide beautiful universe is what it is, just because it is, nothing more. There is no arguing with what is. How can you say that what is, is not? Have you put peace in your pocket so that you can have both hands free to rummage through thoughts and things looking for peace? The only thing that stands between you and peace is the thought that life needs fixing. Accept that life is what it is and you give up the struggle to make it otherwise. What takes the place of struggle is peace. That is it. End of story, end of suffering.

Give it a rest

There is one point that needs to be addressed before we can move along. I know that we started this chapter treating creation as if it has motion and substance. I did that to build a bridge to the next point that must be made in the free will/ determinism debate. And in so doing we will drive the final nail in the coffin of determinism. To do this we have to take a giant step beyond common consciousness, but just for a moment.

You might say that if free will is eliminated then only determinism remains. In a perfect world we have neither. We have already developed this point in chapter 14 but let's do a quick review. Remember the holographic DVD model? (Now stop your groaning.) It depicted the universe as static. It is common consciousness that creates the illusion of movement as if creation were unfolding toward some ultimate and divine end. In actuality, there is no unfolding to be done. Creation is perfectly complete as it is. The existence of objects in motion is an illusion. The universe has nowhere to go and nothing to do. Once you "get it" you too will have nowhere to go and nothing to do. This realization manifests itself as peace. Both free will and determinism are ideas founded on motion. One says we control our actions while the other tells us we do not. In actuality, there is nothing to control. Which means the ideas of free will, determinism and even the idea that neither exist, are just ideas born from illusion. The illusion of motion is created by the sweep of common consciousness across apparent creation. When common consciousness becomes Self-awareness there is no question of controlling or being controlled. One becomes One. And the desire to control or be controlled fades into obscurity in the light of peace.

I know that too much of this kind of abstraction can be discouraging and as I stated earlier I like to build shorter bridges between concepts. But we had to step into the realm beyond movement to pick at the final thread of determinism. Now let's return to more familiar territory and conclude by driving the final nail into the coffin of common consciousness.

Do we do or do we don't?

Every now and again a phrase from a long forgotten song runs through my mind. This one goes "Do we do or do we don't?" I have no idea how it got in there, but it seems to surface from my sub-consciousness when I think about the paradox of the pathless path.

What is the sense of reading this book when I have repeatedly told you that there is no way, no path to peace? And why did it take a whole book to do that? Could you have stopped reading in the first chapter when I first mentioned this? Could you have just read this last chapter and had done with it? There is no knowing except that whatever you do is just right because that is what you did. There has never been a time when you did not do what was perfectly right for the circumstances no matter what you, your mother, your spouse or your boss thinks.

This means that you can do no wrong. Wrong is relative, arbitrary and dependant on interpretation. There are no universal wrongs and when you accept the perfection of what is, there is no question about your actions being right or wrong. In one more way you are free. But there is more.

If you can do no wrong then neither can anyone else. Instead of being told "Love thy neighbor," and struggling with the concept when you have to clean up your yard after your neighbor's dog, you do so effortlessly and completely. The problem arises when localized "me" takes things personally. Then the neighbor is wrong, his dog is wrong and anyone who disagrees with you is wrong and deserving of your wrath.

On the other hand, when you surrender to what is, you still have to clean up the lawn but you do not take it personally. Remember, you can't possibly know what chain of events brought this little present to you. You can know that the driving intelligence and love of the whole of creation is behind it. It is really out of your hands and your neighbor's hands and his dog's, well, paws at least.

The Ten Commandments say do this and don't do that. Your parents, school teachers, friends, family and co-workers say do this and don't do that. Even Kinslow has said do and don't but now he is saying don't do either. The Ten Commandments and the rest are giving relative advice as if it will take you beyond the relative world to eternal salvation. Then Kinslow says that there are no techniques that will give you peace. "Good golly I am so confused," you say as you collapse in a heap at the foot of the altar of bafflement. Take heart, my friend. The final piece to the puzzle of peace is about to be revealed.

It is absolutely true that there are no techniques to lasting peace. That is unless you define "not doing" as a technique. Commonly defined, "technique" is how to do something. But we run into a problem with finding peace because it can only be realized when we stop doing something to find it. That includes looking for it, desiring it or even just thinking about it. The only way you can find peace is to realize that there is nothing you can do to find it. *Once you stop trying and completely accept your life as it is, only then will you be aware of peace's presence.* And that, ladies and gentlemen, is the technique for realizing peace. It is the technique-less technique, the pathless path and the unraveling of the paradox of peace.

When you become self-aware

When you finally and fully accept that you are not in control of your life and settle back in the easy chair of the Self, your life will be much the same as it is now and yet profoundly different. Sure, you will be Self-aware, but what does that mean in the practical terms of day-to-day living? Let's take a look.

How will you act when you become Self-aware? The answer is: In accordance with your genes and upbringing. That's right, basically you will act no differently than you would if you were not Self-aware. True, you may be a little softer, kinder and more loving than before. But don't make the mistake of putting your Self on a pedestal separate from the rest of creation. It is exactly the element of commonness that makes Self sparkle.

I know of Self-aware people who are grumpy, who smoke, are overweight and snore. (Not all the same person.) They love to eat, make love, make money, drive cars and watch television. In short, they are like the rest of us with but a single, subtle and fundamental difference: they are completely accepting of life. This cannot be appreciated by those who suffer. That is why the soft-spoken saint is so revered. She appears to be a product of Self-awareness. But this is not so, not in the way we usually think of it. It is a common misconception that enlightenment changes that person into the slow-talking, slow-walking ever-smiling being unaffected by moods, money or the weather. I would be willing to bet that those Self-aware individuals were slow-talking, slow-walking and ever-smiling before they wholeheartedly accepted what is. We have all known people who are naturally loving and giving because that is just the way they are, just the way their "me" is manifested. When they become Self-aware they will be the same only a little more so.

There is a down side to placing the enlightened above us. It is a practice that frustrates the seeker who tries to emulate the actions of those unique souls in hopes of becoming like them. The gentle ones are no different than their more active, noisy Self-aware peers. But we have turned away from the latter to embrace the former ideal as the poster child for enlightenment. Both types, indeed all Self-aware, are acting in accordance with their genetic makeup molded by the influence of their surroundings. Those of us still struggling with our identity would do well to remember this and leave our preconceived ideas about enlightenment by the side of the road. It is not for their benefit but our own. Believe me, the Self-aware will hardly notice.

In his book *Invitation to Awaken*, the Self-aware Tony Parsons warns, "We should drop any fixed ideas we have about enlightenment, such as the illusory belief that it brings total goodness, bliss and purity. Life simply goes on. Occasionally, I may get angry, feel anxiety...When the contraction passes, I quickly return to an all-encompassing acceptance in which the sense of separateness drops away."

When you awaken to your Self you will still feel anger, anxiety and other familiar emotions. You are still human. You are still bound by the physical and psychological laws that govern all people. Your body/mind will feel everything you felt before and you will accept those feelings unconditionally as being beyond your control, the natural expression of what is.

When you become Self-aware you may find it amusing how many people will not notice. Because they are busy looking to the future or the past, they will miss the present grace that creation is offering them in the form of you. After all, see how many people missed the significance of the man called Jesus while he walked among them. While some look for saviors and others look to dethrone them, you will accept them both as normal expressions of what is.

That brings up an interesting question. When you are Self-aware, can you do something that is wrong? The answer is yes and no. Yes, when seen through the eyes of the uninitiated. They see rights and wrongs everywhere. It is what they do because they break the world into helpful and hurtful pieces, people and events. But through your Self-aware eyes the answer is no. You see only harmony. How, with such vision, could you do anything wrong? The universe will not allow it.

When you become Self-aware, can someone hurt you? Again the answer is yes and no. Obviously you can be hurt physically but you can also be hurt psychologically. What is actually hurt is "me." When Self-aware, you still carry the thin shell of "me" around with you. It is what you used to believe was the genuine you when you lived in the world of pieces. The shell of "me" is like a plastic bell. It reverberates with the words and deeds of man. But those chimes are weak and muffled and can not arouse in you the stronger passions of revenge or greed or guilt. Yours is the silent world of surrender broken only briefly by echoes from your past. No lasting pain can reach into the depths of your silence.

"Me" can be hurt but it only wakes you momentarily to the realization that you are still functioning through a body/mind that is subservient to all laws, natural and man-made. You will feel anger, guilt, anxiety and all manner of desires. But they are only flavors in the wine and will not linger long. They wake you to the joy and the depth of being human.

It is your acceptance of everything as it is that dominates. Any apparently hurtful words or wrongful deeds are acknowledged as part of perfection. There is no need to retaliate against perfection. If your genetically unique, environmentally trained body/mind does defend itself, that is also perfect. When you accept that you have no control then your actions are no longer yours—not that they ever were.

We have been discussing what it is like to be Self-aware. Some Self-aware just popped into that state of total acceptance and that was that. However, most Self-aware souls seem to take their time getting there. It would not be fair to leave you with the impression that the inner light instantly turns on for all of us. In most cases the light of Self-awareness is attached to a dimmer switch that slowly gets brighter over apparent time. I have to say that this is an illusion but one that we should address for those of us who are caught in the "neither fish nor fowl" world between all-out ignorance and being fully Self-aware.

As we begin to accept our world for what it is some very interesting things begin to unfold. For instance, your life will become simultaneously more effortless and more difficult. Difficulties intensify your awareness of pure being. As your awareness of pure being intensifies, your inner and outer lives begin to do battle with each other. In the last chapter of the Bhagavad-Gita (Chapter 18:37), which is an allegory for this struggle between "me" and Self, Krishna addresses this phenomenon when he instructs Arjuna, "That which in the beginning tastes like poison, but turns to nectar in the end—that is the bliss born of a mind at peace with itself."

Jesus also warned us of this spiritual speed bump in the Gospel of Thomas when he said, "Let him who seeks continue seeking until he finds. When he finds, he will become troubled. When he becomes troubled, he will be astonished, and he will rule over the All." These are pretty strong words concerning the tribulations of becoming Self-aware. And Christ would certainly know about trials and tribulations.

Let's take a closer look at what Christ is offering us. It seems we must first seek until we find. That part is simple. We find "it" by being aware of what is. Then Jesus tells us that when we find it we will become "troubled." Now, it's this "troubled" thing I want to look at more closely.

You might say that you already have enough trouble and are not presently looking to add anything more to the list. "When I am ready for more trouble, Frank," you are quick to point out, "you will be the first to know." Fortunately, the day-to-day trouble we commonly experience is not what Jesus is referring to. Our everyday problems are the result of autothinking, seeing pieces where Wholeness reigns. Christ is talking about a different kind of trouble that comes only when we begin to accept what is. What's the difference?

The difference is this. Autothinking troubles make more troubles. Innerthinking clears troubled waters but not without rocking the boat. The trouble Christ makes mention of is the result of purification. If he were talking about the body it would be like giving up caffeine or cigarettes. You feel bad for a few days while the body expels built-up toxins and repairs injured organs and systems. Afterward, free of the toxins, you are healthier and happier. This trouble that Jesus speaks of is purification of a higher kind. When you find "it," by accepting what is, you stop being the actor and become the vehicle through which action is performed. Ego is removed from the equation. Seated in pure being your actions do not make more troubles. Perform a deed while auto-thinking and it will always encourage disharmony. That's right. Even those actions we hold as kind and nurturing, when performed while autothinking will inevitably weaken rather than strengthen. The exact same action performed while innerthinking will always encourage harmony.

Let me underscore that innerthinking or being Self-aware is not a process but a perception. It is the shift from non-acceptance to complete surrender to life as it presents itself to you.

As Self-awareness becomes more prevalent and you become more accepting of what is, things around you will get stirred up. A great deal of rearranging takes place when the field of a powerful magnet influences scattered iron filings, The same will hold true in your life when you grow in peace. The filings that comprise your life, the people, things and events, will go through a great metamorphosis and chaos may well rule the day. Loved ones, friends and coworkers may find your peace a threat to their own efforts to remain in suffering. How they react is a matter of the moment, but react they will. To others you may appear a little odd or unfamiliar. They may not be able to put it into words but your metamorphosis is in some way unsettling to them. They are all iron filings in your field of orderliness. Frank "Kuma" Hewett, author of "The Sacred Waters," wrote, "If you are going to create more light for your world, you must be willing to endure a little heat." Albert Einstein, who had also traveled down this rocky road, said, "Great spirits have always found violent opposition from mediocrities."

I am diagonally parked in a parallel universe

You will begin to feel somehow different. Your old life is also made of iron filings. When the organizing power begins to flow into your relative life, what does not line up with peace will fall away. Your life may alternately be flat and uninteresting, then animated and fresh. It is as if some cosmic hand has rotated your world view two degrees off center. It's the same world from a different perspective. I saw a bumper sticker on a late model Chevy during rush hour traffic the other day. I knew the driver must have been feeling the multidirectional tug of spiritual awakening when she playfully placed it on her tarnished bumper. The sticker tentatively avowed, *I am diagonally parked in a parallel universe*. It could not have been more simply and succinctly stated.

These troubling changes may be subtle or they may be quite noticeable. They may happen quickly or stretch out over a longer period. Or they can descend on you like the proverbial ton of bricks. Your likes and needs will change, your friends may change, your whole life may completely turn on its head. Nothing will be the same for you even if others don't notice a thing.

There is no way of knowing how you will experience this refinement but there is one guiding principle that you can rely on. No matter how much housecleaning takes place it will never be more than you can handle. It will never be stronger than the Self-awareness in which it is taking place. The equation is unequal in favor of peace.

This is the great proving ground. It is an uncomfortable time when the old world has not completely fallen away and yet you have not fully embraced your love of peace. You may feel that you are alone in a wasteland. You may rightly sense that there is no one who understands what you are going through, no one to talk to. This is as it should be as this journey is yours alone. You are learning Self-sufficiency.

This "desolate" period is analogous to the 40 days that Christ spent in the desert. We know that the Devil tempted Christ to turn away from his Self. But what does the Devil represent? What are his temptations? The Devil symbolizes your ego and his temptations are anything that draws your consciousness away from pure awareness. A person who sneaks a cigarette during the uncomfortable purification stage of quitting will then feel immediate relief from withdrawal symptoms. Likewise, when you give into temptation and leave the desert to return to your comfortable old world you may immediately feel a release from the confusion and isolation you may have been feeling. You may succumb to any of your old addictions or embrace new ones. It doesn't matter, for none of your diversions can bring you comfort as they once did. They cannot. As you are beginning to realize, their promise is hollow. As you observe your familiar world crumble around you, your impulse is to save it, repair it so that...The old reasons have no meaning. Meaning has no meaning. Thomas Wolfe is often quoted as saying, "You can never go home again." He's right. Once the light of inner peace begins to dawn, you can no longer hide behind your dreams and hopes. They will have become specters devoid of substance. And as we have already discussed, this is a very good thing.

As a child, I remember singing "Row, Row, Row Your Boat" while riding in the car during our weekly family outing. We sang it as a round, each person starting one line after the other. My father was the conductor, and sitting in the back seat my sister and I were the only two members of this abbreviated choral group. Riding shotgun, my mother refused to lend her voice to our efforts, feeling that someone should keep their eyes on the road. Pop would start the round with one hand keeping time on the wheel while rhythmically pointing at his chest with the other. Then simultaneously wagging his head and his finger, he would turn in his seat and point to each of us when it was our turn to join the song. Mom could be seen alternately looking at my father and the road with a mixture of awe and anxiety, while the three of us blissfully hurtled down the road of perfect harmony. It was not until many years had passed that the profundity of the lyrics struck home. Embedded in this innocent ditty is the formula for living life fully in peace. I would love to know who first sang it to a sleepy-eyed child preparing for the nightly transition from the outer dream to the inner. Sing it again with me, this time with the innocence of a Self-aware adult.

> Row, row, row your boat
> Gently down the stream.
> Merrily, merrily, merrily,
> Life is but a dream.

In time you will begin to realize that your old world is nothing more than a dream. The only reality it ever had was what you gave it. It can not exist on its own, beyond ego. In this desert between heaven and hell your vision begins to clear. You realize that hopes and memories are the stuff of waking dreams. You are ready to let go, to accept what is simply because it is. You are ready to fall in love.

You will be astonished

Once you accept what is, no problem will be more than you can handle. You may doubt it in the beginning but soon will languish in the protective arms of peace while the fury of life rages on without you. You will begin to identify with silence more and activity less. You will wonder why people are getting so upset, and then realize that those same events upset you not so very long ago. Established in your Self, problems are no more than impish children straining at the bonds of convention. They are not good. They are not bad. They just are. You observe the wondrous workings of the universe as it is right now. It is exactly the same as it has always been and yet very different. Now is forever permeated with the indescribable fullness of peace. And as Christ foresaw, you "will be astonished." It is just a small step from being astonished to "ruling over the All."

Ruling over all means accepting what is. Complete acceptance places you beyond the stroke of the sword of suffering. Beyond the reach of your senses, you sense Perfection. You are Perfection. Discovering your Self shimmering silently in the heart of every created thing, you come to know God. You come to know your Self as God.

There is more, for there is more than God. God is defined by His/Her/Its creation. God only exists because creation exists. Beyond God is Nothing. And Nothing is absolute peace. You do not need to understand God or Nothing. You do not need to manage the pieces of your life to know Wholeness. You need only this; to accept what you see. That is the single mantra, the sole sermon of peace. It is just that simple.

Thanks

Well buckaroos, I think that's pretty much all I have to say about happiness, Self-awareness and finding inner peace; at least for now. Before I go, I have something of a personal nature I want to share with you. I have thoroughly enjoyed our time together. On one level we were strangers when we met; two specks of dust passing through a shaft of sunlight, together for awhile. But you are known to me. I know the stillness between your thoughts. It is my stillness, too. You know me in the silence between heartbeats and the space between each breath. The peace that has settled in your soul is the same peace that has settled in mine. I know you as intimately as I know my Self. Beyond the iridescent illusion of life, I know you as my Self. You are the reason I wrote this book and I am very glad to have met you.

MAIN POINTS FOR CHAPTER FIFTEEN

When You Become Enlightened

- Free will is an illusion.

- You do not create your thoughts or actions.

- Thoughts and actions are performed and then "me" takes credit for them.

- Your specific thoughts and actions are the result of your genetic inheritance and environmental imprinting, beyond your control.

- Your genetic inheritance and environmental imprinting were created with the rest of creation.

- Your world, and all of creation, is perfect as it is.

- Enlightenment is nothing more than completely accepting what is, as it is.

Glossary

Autothink—Autothinking is thinking habitually from memory without conscious awareness of the present. When you forget you are thinking and you allow unobserved thoughts to dictate your actions, you are autothinking. It is always outdated and destructive. When you drive your car, during the parts you don't remember you are autothinking. It is the opposite of innerthink.

Bliss—(See pure love.)

Consciousness (Conscious Awareness)—Perception of the relative world without Self-awareness. Autothinking. The apparent flow of pure awareness through the narrow confines of the mind. When consciousness awareness turns inward and becomes aware of Self, it begins innerthinking.

Desire—A desire is ego-driven emotion. It is something you feel you want or need to make some part of you more complete. Desires spring out of memory and bring with them a host of supporting thoughts and emotions. They create action designed to fulfill the desire. That action only creates more and stronger desires.

Ego—Ego arises when mind forgets it is Self. It is the controlling entity of the unaware mind. It is born of fear which is both its foil and its fuel. It wants to be whole and merge with Self but fears assimilation by Self. Ego tries to eliminate what it cannot control. It feels that if it can control everything it can be whole. It is the primal cause of suffering. Time, fear and ego are one and the same. Innerthinking eliminates ego's destructive influence over the mind.

Eu-feelings—Eu-feelings are feelings that are pure and unconditional. They are the natural state of a mind that is aware of its Self. At first, they appear to be hierarchical, but each is a different flavor of Self in the mind. The apparent hierarchy begins with stillness and then evolves to peace, joy, bliss, ecstasy and then complete immersion in the indescribable. Eu-feelings can produce feelings. Feelings cannot produce eu-feelings.

Fear—Fear is the spark that is created when mind separates from Self. Fear is the sum total of all your feelings including happiness and pleasure. It is the primal motivator of the Self-separated mind. Time, fear and ego are one. Innerthinking eliminates fear.

Feelings—Feelings are conditional. All feelings come from the primal feeling fear. Fear creates insecurity which produces the corresponding feeling, thought and action. Feelings are associated with psychological time. When fear manifests in the past it produces feelings of guilt, revenge, self-pity, remorse, sadness, etc. Perceived as the future, fear produces feelings of tension, dread, worry, pride, etc. Anger is the first expression of fear and is also expressed in both the future and the past. Happiness, excitement, delight and even love are fear-based conditional feelings. Feelings can produce other feelings. They cannot produce eu-feelings.

Futurethink—Futurethink is autothinking about the future. You will recognize it by feelings of worry, unease, anxiety, nervousness, tension, dread, stress, pride or may find yourself asking, "What if...happens?"

God—the definition of God changes with the level of consciousness awareness. When experiencing the ultimate sphere of innerthink God is not this or that, God just is. God is pure awareness.

Holographic Consciousness—is pure awareness.

"I"—(See Self)

I Am—(See Self)

Innerthink—The state of thinking, feeling or acting while Self-aware. There are three spheres of innerthinking, one within the other. The innermost sphere is the experience of the observer or witness where awareness is separate from thinking, feeling and acting. In the second sphere the witness starts to lose its separateness as the solidity of thoughts and things begin to soften and take on a friendlier, more caring quality. In the final sphere of innerthink the separateness of the witness is lost as the outer and inner worlds merge in pure awareness. There are three main advantages of innerthinking—(1) decreases negative energy, (2) weakens ego's influence, (3) strengthens awareness of Self.

Intuition—the expression of Self in the phenomenal world. Innerthinking. (Synonymous with "Wisdom.")

Knowing—When Self becomes aware of itself that is Knowing. The transition from knowing to Knowing is innerthinking. Knowing tenderly nurtures, guides and protects us. This is what we call intuition. Intuition is the tender expression of the Self reflected in the mind. Intuition is Knowing without analysis and logic while it enriches and supports both. Intuition is Knowing that Nothing has everything under control.

Knowledge—Knowledge is the result of gathering data which adds to our understanding. Knowledge is a synthesis of understanding and experience. It is relative and changes with time and circumstances. Knowledge is ignorance.

"Me"—Everything that makes a person unique is "me." "Me" is made of thoughts and emotions, experiences, memories hopes and fears. "Me" changes over your lifetime.

Momentum—The state where inner peace is automatically reestablished when it is lost.

Nothing—Nothing cannot be understood. Nothing is not empty. Nothing is not separate from what It creates. It is Its creation. Everything is Nothing. Nothing only appears as the phenomenal world. Self is Nothing. To know Self is to know Nothing which is to Not-Know.

Not-Knowing—Not-Knowing is awareness of Nothing. When Self drops away leaving only pure awareness, that is Not-Knowing. The advantage of the Not-Knower is that of knowing no movement and no other. No movement means It is timeless and no other means It is One. Not-Knowing has nowhere to go and nothing to do. The illusion of going and doing has been exposed. It is free to be. Not-Knowing is the realization of absolute unity. (See Pure Awareness.)

Observe—(See Witness)

Pastthink—When the mind is autothinking in the past. You will recognize it by feelings of guilt, regret, resentment, sadness, self-pity, bitterness, non-forgiveness or grief.

Pure Awareness—The highest realization. Awareness of that which is unchanging, without beginning or end. The progenitor and substance of all form. Pure awareness realizes that creation is an illusion. It is pure intelligence, being and love. (See Not-Knowing.)

Pure Being—Pure being is pure awareness. Since pure awareness is everywhere at once it does not move and is therefore pure being.

Pure Consciousness—awareness of no-thinking, the gap between thoughts.

Pure Love—Pure love is pure awareness. Awareness that falls equally on all things, sees no opposites, has no point of view and creates no disharmony.

Psychological Time—Psychological time is the cause of all the problems facing human kind. The mind that is not aware of the present vacillates between the past and future, neither of which exists. This vacillation creates the illusion of movement we call time. Problems arise when we mistake the illusion for the truth. The mind firmly set on the present is at rest, breaking the illusion of movement and removing the cause of suffering.

Self—Self is unbounded and beyond time. It is aware without movement. Self is a wave, created on the silent ocean of pure awareness when there is something to observe. When it becomes aware of its own existence, it becomes aware of pure love. The symptom of consciousness becoming aware of Self is inner peace. It is the unchanging part of you that was there in childhood, adolescence and adulthood, watching but never interfering, untouched but supporting all that you are. In the beginning it is the silent witness of your life. In the end, the wave of Self realizes that there is nothing to observe but Self and settles back into the ocean of pure awareness.

Self-Awareness—awareness of that unbounded, eternal aspect of life upon which the mind/body/environment is built. In its simplest state it is recognized as the gap between thoughts. Complete realization of Self comes upon its dissolution into pure awareness. At this point, no separate Self can be observed as all things are equal in their expression of pure awareness.

Spiritual—The perception of wholeness; innerthinking.

Surrender—Surrender means we relinquish hope and are not looking to the future for things to get better. It is not "giving up." It means opening our awareness to Self and waiting to see what options will issue forth from that state of infinite possibilities. Surrender recognizes Self as the answer to all problems.

Wisdom—the expression of Self in the phenomenal world. Innerthinking. (Synonymous with "Intuition.")

Witness—The witness is a door through which common consciousness must go to find pure awareness. The witness is the Self. In the early stages, the witness is distinctly separate from objects and activity. In the later stages, the witness begins to recognize the stillness of Self in objects and activity. Finally, the witness loses its individuality and merges into pure awareness. (Synonymous with "Observe.")

Bibliography

Ainsworth, Vaune and George Land. *Forward to Basics*. D.O.K Publishers, Inc, 1982

Balsekar, Ramesh. *Peace and Harmony in Daily Living*. Mumbai, India, Yogi Impressions. 2003
Balsekar, Ramesh. *The Ultimate Understanding*. Watkins, New York. 2002

Barnet, Lincoln. *The Universe and Dr. Einstein*. Mentor, New York. 1952

Bohm, David. *Thought as a System*. Routledge, 1994
Bohm, David. *Wholeness and the Implicate Order*. Ark Paperbacks, London. 1980
Bohm, David and B.J. Hiley. *The Undivided Universe*. Routledge, London. 1993
Bohm, David and Lee Nichols(Eds). *On Dialogue*. Routledge, London. 1996

Braden, Gregg. *The Isaiah Effect, Decoding the Last Science of Prayer & Prophecy*. Harmony Books, 2000

Briggs, John and Peat, David F. *Seven Life Lessons of Chaos: Spiritual Wisdom From the Science of Change*. Harper Perennial, New York. 2000

Capra, Fritjof. *The Web of Life: A New Scientific Understanding of Living Systems*. Anchor, New York. 1996
Capra, Fritjof. *The Turning Point: Science, Society, and the Rising Culture*. New York: Bantam, New York 1983
Capra, Fritjof. *The Tao of Physics*. Bantam, New York. 1976

Chopra, Deepak. *How to Know God*. Harmony Books, New York. 2000
Chopra, Deepak. *The New Physics of Healing*. Sounds True Recording, Boulder, CO. 1990 Audiocassette

Coleman, James. *Relativity for the Layman*. Signet. New York. 1958

De Mello, *Anthony. Awareness: The Perils and Opportunities of Reality.* Doubleday, New York. 1992

Einstein, Albert. *Relativity: The Special and the General Theory.* Crown Publishers, New York. 1961

Gilovich, Thomas. *How We Know What Isn't So: The Fallibility of Human Reason In Everyday Life.* Free Press, New York. 1991

Gleick, James. Chaos: *Making a New Science.* Viking, New York. 1988

Goldsmith, Joel. *Practicing the Presence.* Harper Collins, New York. 1958

Harding, Douglas. *Look For Yourself.* Inner Directions, Carlsbad, CA.1998

Land, George. *Grow or Die. The Unifying Principle of Transformation.* John Wiley and Sons. 1997
Land, George and Jarman, *Beth. Breakpoint and Beyond, Mastering the Future Today.* Leadership 2000 Press, 2000

Leider, Richard J. *The Power of Purpose, Creating Meaning In Your Life and Work.* MJF Books, New York. 1997

Mitchell, Stephen. *Tao Te Ching.* Harper Perennial, New York. 1991

Mahesh Yogi, Maharishi. *On The Bhagavad-Gita: A New Translation and Commentary.* Penguin, Maryland, USA. 1969
Mahesh Yogi, Maharishi. *The Science of Being and Art of Living.* International SRM Publications, London. 1963

Nisargadatta, Maharaj. *I Am That.* Acorn Press. Durham, NC. 1973

O'Connor, Joseph and Ian McDermott. *The Art of Systems Thinking, Essential Skills For Productivity and Problem Solving.* Thorsons, 1997

Parsons, Tony. *Invitation To Awaken.* Inner Directions, Carlsbad, CA. 2004

Renz, Karl. *The Myth of Enlightenment.* Inner Directions, Carlsbad, CA. 2005

Russell, Bertrand. *The ABC of Relativity.* Signet, New York. 1958

Russell, Peter. *The Global Brain Awakens, Our Next Evolutionary Leap*. Global Brain Inc., Palto Alto, CA 1995

Tolle, Eckhart. *The Power of Now*. New World Library. Novato, CA. 1999
Tolle, Eckhart. *Silence Speaks*. New World Library, Novato, CA. 2003

Wheatly, Margaret J. *Leadership and the New Science. Discovering Order in a Chaotic World*. Berrett-Koehler Publishers, San Francisco. 1999

Wheatly, Margaret J, and Myron Kellner-Rogers.*A Simpler Way*. Barrett-Koehler Publishers, San Francisco. 1996

Woodroffe, John. Is' *Opanisad*. Vedanta Press, Madras, India. 1971

Frank welcomes your comments and questions.
He can be contacted at:
Toll Free: 877-811-5287
Website:www.QuantumEntrainment.com
E-mail: info@QuantumEntrainment.com
Mailing Address: PO Box 1774
Sarasota, Florida 34230-1774

LucidSea

LaVergne, TN USA
22 July 2010
190484LV00004B/134/P